WHEN DUTY CALLED: EVEN GRANDMA HAD TO GO

by
Dianah Kwiatkowski
as told to Sandra Warren

Remember Our Troops

Dianah Kwiatkowski

To Barb,
Enjoy Dianah's Story!
Thank a veteran for your
freedom!
Sandra Warren

Silk Label Books

Unionville, New York

Disclaimer

The events documented in this story are factual, recounted as I remember living them. However, the names of those with whom I interacted in the military and at home have been changed to protect their privacy. They know who they are.

"Dianah,
Your story is of the lightness meeting the dark, of the grit and courage of kindness overcoming oppression, not really by force but simply because the light dares to exist, and to say, in the abyss of grandeur of the blackness, 'Behold, I am.' The Saudi world will never be the same because once a door is created, it always exists. You and others like you have opened a portal in the darkness and left a light that once seen in the soul, can never be extinguished."
Stephanie Emily Schwertner

Silk Label Books
First Avenue, PO Box 700
Unionville, NY 10988-0700
(845) 726-3434
FAX: (845) 726-3824
email: rfpress@frontiernet.net

ISBN: 1-928767-34-6

Printed and bound in the United States of America on recycled, acid-free paper using vegetable based inks and environmentally-friendly cover coatings by Royal Fireworks Printing Co., of Unionville, New York.

It's not often that a forty-seven-year-old woman from the suburbs, in pursuit of an advanced degree, finds herself in Saudi Arabia in the middle of a war. But I did. I did it to myself by joining the Army Reserves in September of 1990. The experience changed me and every facet of my life.

I felt compelled to share the story that you are about to read. I share it in hopes that it will challenge your spirit never to give up when things get tough, not to be afraid to seek out opportunities that may seem unreachable or impossible. The biggest lesson I learned by serving as a nurse during the Persian Gulf War is that with God's help we can do anything.

Captain Dianah Kwiatkowski

Cleveland, Ohio

August, 1999

ACKNOWLEDGMENTS

Thankfulness to the almighty Jesus, to my family and friends who were always present in spirit and thoughts, Southwest General Medical Center, St. Adalbert Catholic Church and all Christians that prayed and thought of all the military during Desert Storm.

Cleveland, Ohio

Captain Dianah Kwiatkowski August, 1999

From the writer:

I offer my sincere thanks to Dianah Kwiatkowski for giving me the opportunity to share her story. Together we waded through hours of cassette tapes piecing together her many experiences as an Army Reserve Nurse.

Thank you also to the many people who supported my efforts by reading drafts and making suggestions: Debra Sharp who helped with editing early on and Terese Campbell whose constant encouragement, editorial expertise and creative genius helped shape the final draft. Thank you also to my family: my husband Roger and daughters Kerri, Leslie and Michelle.

Sandra Warren

Cleveland, Ohio August, 1999

I now understand why veterans, Vietnam veterans in particular, stay locked in the past. To separate it from the present is difficult. A smell, sand on a beach on a rainy afternoon, a loud unexpected noise, the drone of airplanes overhead, the flap-flap-flap of an awning, the wap-wap-wap of a low flying helicopter; the slightest thing can take you back. In the blink-of-an-eye it all comes rushing back, and you are there, again. The fear, the loneliness, the disbelief, the terror of not knowing from moment-to-moment if you will live or die, is overwhelming. It takes every ounce of control to force yourself to believe that you are home and safe. Then, guilt rolls in, and you feel as if you are losing your mind. Shouldn't you be able to control yourself?

People around you, even those who love and support you, can't understand. Mood swings, irritability, irrational behavior are all a part of it. Vietnam vets suffer because of the lack of support from the American people upon their return and the lack of knowledge in the medical field at the time, coupled with the horrors they experienced. Persian Gulf War vets suffer for different reasons. They can't claim lack of support. All came home to a "Hero's Welcome." In fact, some suffer from embarrassment, because they felt the adulation undeserved. Others suffer because of the perception the general population received from television and the media; the perception that the war was an air war fought primarily by the air force. The ground war, after all, in fact the entire war, only lasted 21 days. What could be so traumatic about that?

But, it was traumatic, traumatic for all who were there. There was the fear of the unknown; a strange place, with strange customs; living in tents; fighting difficult, unfamiliar terrain and extreme climatic conditions; feeling untrained and physically unprepared for the labor-intense jobs all shared; watching missiles destroyed overhead; seeing, smelling and experiencing the effects of burning oil wells visible on the horizon; and dealing with the terror and fear that at any moment a missile could spew its deadly load and all would be lost. Unlike other wars, in the Persian Gulf War there was no "front." Anyone and anything over there was a target for immediate demise.

I believe that everyone who served in the Persian Gulf War suffers from "Post Traumatic Stress." I'm sure of it; and know especially about the medical personnel. They were the ones who, in addition to injured Americans and allies, had to deal with the thousands of Iraqi prisoners-of-war (POW's), many of whom had symptoms of severe starvation and disease in addition to serious injuries, suffered when shot from behind by their own men—Saddam's Republican Guard. These POW's had been brainwashed to hate Americans and loath American women. It was extremely difficult for caring, well-trained professionals to work hard to save the lives of men who would never be grateful, who fought their every administrations, and who would kill their caretakers at a moment's notice if given the opportunity.

A tragedy of this pressure is that among the medical staff, who should have been most aware of Post Traumatic Syndrome and its effects, few are getting help. Post Traumatic Stress doesn't go away on its own.

How do I know?

I am a nurse and I was there.

This is a part of my story.

CHAPTER ONE

"A man's mind plans his way, but the Lord directs his step."

Proverbs 16 Verse 9

Tension hung heavy, taut like a rubber band stretched beyond limits. In the auditorium floated an aura of expectation. Morning chatter ceased mid-sentence as one by one, 400 Army Reserve doctors and nurses entered and sat down.

Colonel Smith, normally calm and cool, paced anxiously. Glancing at the rapidly filling room, he checked his watch and paced some more. There was a nervous cadence to his steps, programmed through years in the military. My eyes, alert and alarmed, followed his every movement. Back and forth, back and forth, stop, check watch, look around, back and forth.

Goose bumps dotted my arms. Shuddering, I sat down on the cold folding chair and looked around. Little things, subtle changes, caught my eye. The table was still piled high with handouts, scattered notes, an overhead projector and a water glass, but next to the podium now stood the American flag that yesterday graced the edge of the stage.

The focus of the morning class was to be map reading and the use of the compass: how to shoot an isthmus off a compass and how to direct yourself if you got lost, to be exact. I had enjoyed the previous navigational lesson, and I was looking forward to learning more. Were we still to learn map reading?

We were two days away from our final day of Officer Basic Training (OBT). It was assumed orders would be given on that final day. Rumors had been flying for several days about when it might happen and what those orders might be. Apparently there was some truth to the rumors this time. *Jesus, Mary and Joseph!*

Leaning forward, I looked down the row at Grady. She shrugged her shoulders as if to say, "So, what now?" Returning her shrug I motioned "Who knows?" followed by a thumbs up, our signal for "hang tough...keep the faith...we can do this...survival." I knew we are thinking the same thing. *What ever they have to tell us, I hope they keep it short and sweet.*

Sitting back, I returned my gaze to the colonel, noticing his formal attire for the first time. *Class A uniform. Oh, God! This is it. We're going to be told today!* My hand unconsciously reached for the medal around my neck as I uttered a quick prayer. "Jesus, Mary and Joseph, help me to accept what is about to happen. Give me strength, Oh Lord." Crossing myself, I took a deep breath and willed myself to be calm.

My edginess seemed shared as I watched the entering reservists respond to the change in the colonel and the things that had been added to the stage. A strained silence filled the room.

The growing sense of alarm in the auditorium wasn't new. It had been building daily. Through weapons training, I could feel it. Through chemical and biological warfare training, I could feel it. Nuclear training took its toll, and now this. Collective emotion, almost unbearable in a group, frustration, exhaustion, anticipation, fear, all emotional responses typical of those out of their element thrown together by circumstance. All this training for support service in a backup hospital seemed extreme. It was frustrating. As doctors and nurses,

2

we were take-charge people being led through a maze of information leading to, we knew not where.

As the clock struck 0900, a door near the stage burst open. In walked a giant of a man, six feet, five inches at least, maybe taller, also dressed in formal attire. It was a general but not just any general. It was the general in charge of all the reserve medical units in the United States! *This is serious stuff. Jesus, Mary and Joseph, give me strength! Give me strength!* I prayed over and over as rapidly as I could.

"Attention!" snapped the colonel in the most aggressive, authoritative tone we had heard all week. We jumped to our feet.

We all stood, riveted as statues, for the first time really looking like soldiers.

It seemed to take forever for the general to reach the stage. He mounted the stairs, every movement precise and deliberate. After saluting the colonel, he turned, removed the briefcase from under his arm and placed it on the podium. Taking one last drag on the cigar hanging from his lips, his emotionless eyes scanned the group. He acknowledged our salute with a nod of his head.

"Good morning!"

"Good morning, sir!" echoed the officers in unison.

"At ease. You may be seated."

The room became quiet...very quiet, very fast. Four hundred pairs of eyes were riveted on the uniform at the podium. Then the general, with great dramatic flare, extended his arm, index finger pointed directly at us. Slowly, he turned, sweeping his finger across the audience from one side of the room to the other. His finger seemed to touch each one of us as his voice boomed into the microphone, "All of you, in this room, are going to Saudi Arabia!"

And this was how I, a forty-seven year old grandmother from middle America, an experienced RN, yet, newly inducted, untrained army reservist, found myself on my way to Saudi Arabia to serve in what became known as the Persian Gulf War.

CHAPTER TWO

"There's a divinity that shapes our ends. Rough-hew them how we will."

Shakespeare, HAMLET

It really began three months earlier with my decision to enlist in the army reserves. I had contemplated enlisting for a long while, but the illness and subsequent death of my mother had delayed my commission for almost a year. My mother's family was extremely political, opinionated and pro-American; democratic through and through. Lively political discussions were a major part of all family gatherings, usually led by my uncle, then a senator in Pennsylvania. For generations, every male in the family had served in the military. While growing up, I'd listened to uncles tell tales of their experiences in World War II and Korea. As a young girl I envied them and fantasized about joining the military and serving my country, too. Now, more than thirty years later, I would get that chance.

I'll admit that my main attraction to the army reserves was the financial support package for higher education. After working in the intensive care unit of our local hospital for many years, at forty-seven, I thought it was time to move on. Thoughts of changing direction and teaching in a nursing school began to haunt me. The idea of sharing with the next generation of care-givers my experience, knowledge and love, held great appeal. But to teach I needed an advanced degree.

In August of 1990, a telephone call came from a recruiter anxious for my decision. With a husband, five children and four grandchildren, it wasn't my decision alone to make. Their feelings had to be considered. My husband, Tom, and I discussed it at great length. Could he handle the homefront during the occasional mandatory weekend retreats and the three week summer camp? What if I were to be deployed? Could he handle an extended absence? What about the kids? Could everyone handle living with an army officer? We weighed and counter-weighed the options. We prayed about it. Together with God's help, we came to a decision. I called the recruiter.

The recruiter arrived with pamphlets to read and papers to sign. Only one burning question separated me from signing on the doted line. "What if the U.S. entered a war, what would the responsibilities of the medical corps be?" I inquired.

The recruiter's answer was most firm and reassuring. "The Army Reserve Medical Corps is just that...a reserve corps; support personnel which, if deployed, would be utilized in hospitals within the United States or at hospitals in back-up countries, far removed from conflict. There are enough enlisted medical personnel to handle more immediate needs," he ended.

With his assurance, I carefully signed the official document.

Mid-September, 1990, in the living room of my home, I was commissioned a Second Lieutenant in the United States Army Reserves and assigned to the 350th EVAC Hospital Unit operating out of Canton, Ohio. A commissioned officer administered the oath while Tom and four of our children looked on. It was a proud moment. When the bars were pinned to my uniform, I felt like a circle had been completed.

Had I really understood then what I know now, I wouldn't have been surprised later by my deployment placement. An EVAC hospital unit (an evacuation unit) is a hospital setup in a war theater. I was a brand-new recruit and ignorant of military terminology. Make no mistake. I joined the army reserve for the educational benefits and to serve my country. There was never any doubt that I would have to serve in a military hospital if deployed. What I didn't understand was that deployment could be in a military hospital in a potential war zone.

In the midst of my decision to join the army reserves, Tom and I were notified that our son, Dave, a lieutenant in the navy, was being sent to the Persian Gulf. Iraq had invaded Kuwait a few weeks earlier and was systematically demolishing the country. United States troops were being sent to join other United Nations troops to stop the destruction. My son, my child, was being sent into a potential war zone!

Terror filled me every time I thought about my son in the Persian Gulf. My normally strong composure, toughened by years of counseling families and patients dealing with life-threatening trauma in the intensive care ward, began to crack. This was different. This was *my* child!

Tom was becoming concerned with my behavior. I hadn't realized it was noticeable. "Maybe you should find someone to talk to," he suggested. His concern shook me into action.

Through connections at the hospital, I heard about a support group recently formed for families whose loved ones were being sent to the Persian Gulf. I was skeptical, yet needy. How many times had I counseled families to seek the support of others? "Join a support group somewhere, they can help you," I would advise. Now it was time to take my own advice. I decided to give an outside group a try, just once.

Meetings were held in the YMCA building in a neighboring community, every other week. Expecting to slip into a back row seat and blend into a crowd, I instead walked into a meeting of six other individuals, one a reporter, sitting in the back of the room seemingly taking notes. It was only the second time the group had gotten together.

The small size of the group concerned me at first, but it turned out to be an advantage. It forced a more intimate, personal experience. One by one each person shared his or her story. Seven strangers were brought together by the pain of separation and the threat of war.

"My son has been sent to the Persian Gulf, and we don't know where he is," I declared. "There is this feeling growing inside of me, uncontrollable and frightening. 'War fever,' I call it. Does anyone else know what I mean?" Heads nodded in understanding. "How do I deal with this? What should I do?" Averted stares and silence followed. No one had the answers that night, but when people come together with common concerns, somehow, support does happen. I was glad that I went.

The reporter sent by local media sat quietly in the back of the room, occasionally scratching words into his spiral notebook. When we adjourned, he came forward and asked of no one in particular, "How do you feel about your loved one being deployed?" His question silenced the chatter. All heads turned to gaze at him. He stood there, pen hovering over pad, poised to begin. I stared at him, wondering what he had been doing the last hour.

At first, no one said a word. Then, from somewhere deep inside me came an understanding and an answer. He wrote furiously as I began. "You want to know how I feel?" He nodded, oblivious to my fury. "Well, I'll tell you how I feel. Now I know what every mother has felt since the beginning of time, when her child is called to war. Whether the Civil War, the Spanish-American War, World War I or II, Korea, or Vietnam, whatever the war, there is this void, this vacuum...a deep concern for your own child and the sons and daughters of all the others." Pausing, I willed the reporter to look up. He wouldn't. "We're scared to death! We want our loved ones home safe! That's how we feel!" I concluded irritated. My eyes bore into him. He turned abruptly, unwilling to meet my gaze, muttered a feeble "thanks" and hurriedly exited the room.

October brought falling leaves and my first official drill as an Army Reserve Officer. Pride mixed with worry engulfed me as I changed into my camouflage duds. "Did I have them on right?" Tom leaned against the bedroom door smiling. "You look spectacular my dear," he said.

"Is that anyway to talk to an officer?" I barked in my best mock Army voice.

"Excuse me, Lieutenant, ma'am," he responded jumping to attention.

"Oh, Tom, does it really look alright? The recruiter didn't given me any instructions when I picked it up. Maybe there aren't any or maybe this is the army's way of initiating new recruits," I joked, nervously. "I guess I'll find out soon enough."

"Stop worrying. You look terrific. If there had been any instructions, they would have told you," he said trying to reassure me.

"Well, everything looks like it's on right," I said aloud to the officer in the mirror, all the while thinking, *the Class A dress uniform won't be as easy. I'll have to find someone to instruct me before the next drill.*

Reflected in the mirror in the foyer stood an Army officer ready for drill. The face was familiar, but a new role had emerged. I was no longer just wife, mother, grandmother, and nurse. Second Lieutenant, Army Reserve had been added. I saluted, gave Tom a quick kiss and turned towards the door. It creaked as I stepped over the threshold onto the porch and hurried toward my car. *Oh, God. No turning back now. Jesus, Mary and Joseph, what have I done?*

Driving towards the drill hall, every war movie I had ever watched skipped through my head. Memories of uncles sitting around my grandparent's table exchanging military stories popped in and out. Expectations of strict discipline, strict dress codes, orderly conduct, highly regimented and regulated procedures occupied my thoughts. How would I ever adjust?

Upon my arrival, no one seemed to know what to do with me. Apparently I was dressed correctly because no one said a thing about that. The person assigned to lead me around and make sure that I became involved was very casual. Nothing was as I had imagined.

The focus for the evening involved the M-16 rifle. As we moved through the lesson, I became more appreciative of my father's insistence, when I was a child, that I learn how to clean, load and shoot a shotgun. It was an experience that

I could draw on. Taking apart and putting together the M-16 rifle, although different, had many similarities.

It was at this first drill that I met Donna Grady, a fiery red head wearing glasses that barely hid her mischievous blue eyes. We were drawn to each other immediately: similar age, similar backgrounds, older children and husbands at home. She worked at Lorain Community Hospital, about thirty miles west of Berea, the town where I live. We had much in common.

Unlike me, however, Grady was a perfectionist. That was obvious from the get-go. She was so funny about everything, especially her uniform. "Are my pants wrinkled? I hate wrinkles!" she would complain daily. I loved to tease her about it. With her, everything had to be just so. My philosophy, on the other hand was, as long as you've got it on, that's enough! One might say my approach was a more "comfortable" one. It's not that I was sloppy, or didn't care about my appearance, it just wasn't that important to me.

Strong friendships were critical during deployment. It wasn't enough to have loving support at home, you needed someone to laugh with, to cry with, to be serious with...someone willing to "get-in-your-face" and snap you out of the waves of depression that came too often. Grady became that person for me. Little did we know at that first drill how our lives would intertwine during the next few months.

The support group met again, and this time the room was packed. Sixty-six units from Ohio had been called up for duty. My status within the support group had changed since the first meeting. Now, I was not only a mother seeking the support of others in the same situation, but also a member and representative of the very establishment that had called their wives,

11

husbands, sons and daughters to prepare for war. Everyone wanted to know what was happening. "What have you been told?" they asked. I had to admit that I knew nothing in terms of deployment. I reminded them that I'd just joined and that I'd been to only one drill. "But, surely you know something more," one particularly distraught woman pressed. "I wish I did," I replied. "We'll be the last to know. I will tell you this, though, I'm extremely impressed with the caliber of nurses and doctors in my unit. They're highly trained with years of experience. I'm confident that they will be able to handle any emergency. Your loved ones, if need be, will get the best medical attention possible!" My words of assurance seemed to help her.

The November drill was more formal than the first. Class A uniforms were required. The entire unit was there. Chairs were arranged in perfect rows with special seats designated for high ranking officers, separate from the platoon. The order of business was deployment...the "what ifs" and the "how tos." We made lists of things to take and things to leave behind, essentials to fill a duffel bag...underwear, toiletries, clothes, etc. The technical aspects dealing with making wills, canceling insurance policies and signing over financial responsibility to a family member, were covered. All these things were necessary when deployed.

I tried to ignore the queasy feeling in my stomach. I thought, *well, okay, do what you have to do, learn all you can. Having this knowledge is an important and necessary part of military life. Standard procedure. Besides, if it's God's will...But surely, God isn't going to send a grandmother like me to war,* I rationalized. *It is important to be prepared, though, just in case.*

The next day we joined our unit in Canton, Ohio, for regular duties. I still didn't know what regular duties were expected of me. No one had bothered to tell me. It was a real "feel-out" phase. The handbook, *Military Qualifications II: Manual of Common Tasks,* helped some. I learned prioritizing and resource tasks for training, training management and what you were going to do that day; for example, train a 91 Charlie (LPN) how to start an intravenous drip (IV) or to draw blood or set traction, that kind of thing. By the end of the day I had finally figured out that my major role as an officer was going to be to teach. How ironic was that!

The weekend before Thanksgiving I pulled several twelve hour shifts at the hospital. On Saturday, my friend Pauline came running up to me looking surprised.

"Dianah, what are you doing here?"

"What do you mean? I told you last week that I was on this weekend."

"Yes. But..."

"But what?" I asked.

"I just assumed that when your unit is called up, you need to go right away," she said.

"Where'd you get the idea my unit was called up?"

"I heard it on the news!" she said.

"No you didn't!"

"Oh, yes I did. Last night. They said the 350th had been called up."

"This isn't funny, Pauline. You're making me mad," I said, angrily.

"Fine. Don't believe me. I wouldn't kid about something this serious, Dianah. I thought you knew me better than that." Furious, she turned and hurried down the hall.

My heart was pounding as I approached the nurses' station. I went right to the phone and called home. Tom answered after three rings. I started talking as soon as I heard him pick up the receiver.

"Tom...Pauline said she heard that the 350th was called up. Did you hear anything? Did I get any phone calls? Did anyone from the reserves call?"

"What?" he asked surprised. "Calm down Di! No, I didn't hear anything."

"Have you been watching the news?"

"Yes, hon. It's been on. I'm sure Pauline is mistaken. If she isn't...well, we'll hear soon enough."

"But, Tom. What if it's tr..."

"Don't borrow trouble, Di. Let's not worry about it until we have to. Look. I'll call the kids and see if they've heard anything. You go back to work and don't think about it. Okay?"

"Yeah, right. I'll try. Thanks, Tom....Love you." I put the receiver down slowly, trying to absorb the possibility. *They won't send me,* I thought to myself. *I'm too old. I'm too new. I don't know anything about the military.* Just then a patient call button began to ring. I grabbed the chart and hurried off towards the room.

The rest of the evening I asked everyone I saw if they had heard anything. They all said, no! The next day I got the same response. Nobody had heard anything except Pauline, who swore that she'd heard it again, that morning. On Monday I heard it myself and called my unit.

"Hello, this is Lieutenant Kwiatkowski."

"Report immediately!" came the orders. The matter-of-fact response knocked the breath out of me. The chair caught me as my hand, visibly shaking, hung up the phone. *Jesus, Mary and Joseph!*

This is nuts! I'm brand new, a beginner. I've only drilled twice for God's sake! I know nothing about being in the military! My mind bounced around. I began talking to myself. *How am I going to tell Tom? The kids?* My thoughts became irrational, then rational, then cocky. *I've been a nurse for a hundred years, and I've seen it all. I can handle anything!* Cockiness always helped me rationalize my way into accepting most anything. I can be really cocky. Now, on my feet and pacing, I continued my conversation with myself. *Hey, I wonder where they'll send me....East coast? ....West coast?....I've always wanted to live in California.... Didn't the recruiter say, 'Reserve units will be used stateside.' I can't think. Where are the Army hospitals in the U.S.?.... Maybe it won't be so bad.* The pacing continued. Then panic set in, again. *Why me, God?* I prayed, *Why me? I'm old! I'm a grandmother! Grandmothers don't get called up! This has to be a mistake. What did I do? Why are you letting this happen to me so soon? I'm not prepared.* I waited for an answer, a sign, reassurance, anything. Nothing came.

The 350th EVAC Hospital unit was mobilized. I was being deployed and there was nothing I could do about it. I knew the risk when I signed, but never in my wildest dreams did I think it would happen this soon.

○   ○   ○

The next few days were a whirlwind. I went back and forth to headquarters at least a hundred times, it seemed, trying to get my records in order. Lines, lines, endless lines slowly moving from station to station. Each station a table. Each table designated to handle particular aspects of my life. One helped me write my last will and testament and power of attorney. My insurance had to be cancelled or the company would cancel it for me. Health records were checked and double-checked. Arrangements for my army pay were made...direct deposit only into accounts, no checks would be sent home. Dependents were checked and double checked. Medical records, shots, so many things to do. Like nursing school. Do this...don't ask why! Hundreds of people trying to get their lives in order before leaving for their ordered destinations.

The military machine works swiftly when necessary. It was amazing how quickly our unit was mobilized. They needed to get us into a military environment and a military mindset as quickly as possible; an environment where intensive training could take place. The training was essential even though we were backup support medical personnel. None of us ever considered the possibility that our destination might be somewhere outside of the United States and involve white sand and the hot, blazing sun.

Happy Thanksgiving! What a bummer!

In the middle of all this my family was in limbo, not quite believing what was happening. Everyone was reacting from within his and her own instability, and I wasn't much help because of my own.

My son David was already in the Persian Gulf. Patrick, Becky and Mary were still at home. Jackie lived close by with her husband and four children.

Mary is the silent type, often holding in feelings that should be expressed. She had just started her senior year in high school. I knew she was scared about what was coming down the road, but I couldn't help her. I felt incapacitated just trying to deal with my own feelings about it. It tore me apart to think that I wouldn't be sharing these important months with her. I tried not to think about what I would miss. She would have to rely on her older sisters this time.

Between trips to headquarters, Tom and I drove Becky to college in Pennsylvania. We helped her get set up in her apartment and hurried back to Cleveland. Becky was in the naval reserves so she understood my commitment and my responsibility to follow orders. Even so, she was upset.

The grandchildren were just too young to understand. They thought I was going on a big trip. But their mom, Jackie, knew and was having difficulty accepting it. She cried a lot. She was having a hard time with the "what ifs." What if Mom never comes back? I think she wanted to make amends for things she had done as a young woman that I didn't approve of, set the record straight, clear the slate. We all felt that way. I certainly wasn't going to leave with anything important left unsaid.

Patrick is the philosopher in the family, very rational and political. He believes strongly in justice and the American way. Like Becky, he was supportive and believed it was my

17

responsibility to go. If he was afraid or concerned, he never let me know.

I knew my husband would be okay. Tom is strong and very faithful. He had been in the military, the 3rd Armored Division. Even so, he felt inadequate trying to relate to me as a military person. Prayer and a belief in Jesus Christ have been the foundation of our marriage, so I had to trust that the Lord would see him...see us all through this.

People asked if there were things I could do to get out of my obligation. I suppose there were, but the thought never crossed my mind. Intellectually, I felt honored to exercise my skills as a professional nurse, to help American and allied forces. Emotionally, though, I was scared to death. I had always taught my children that it was a privilege to be an American; that getting involved and giving back was an obligation that we all have. I could never have lived with myself or faced them if I wrangled my way out of this responsibility.

That I was "active duty," that the government had control over my life, hadn't sunk in yet. All through deployment preparations, I was allowed to go home at night. It felt like any other job during busy times.

Fourteen nurses in our unit had not completed Officer Basic Training (OBT). I was one of them. Consequently, after spending a wonderful Thanksgiving day with my family, I boarded a plane bound for Fort Sam Houston, in San Antonio, Texas.

Things happened so fast. One minute I was a middle-class housewife, mother, grandmother, nurse, and the next minute I was off to Officer Basic Training (OBT), the medical version of Boot Camp!

As the airplane rolled down the runway, I patted the rosary tucked in my breast pocket and clutched the cross and the new medal of the Blessed Mother, hanging on a chain around my neck. It had appeared that morning on my dresser. I don't remember ever having seen it before. I held onto them as if my life depended on them. Several times in the last few minutes I asked myself, "is this real?" My emotions were in a jumble.

The situation though foreign, seemed very familiar; like when my mother put me on a bus for summer camp, as a child. The feelings were the same; excitement about the adventure ahead yet fear about leaving home. This time though, the fear was adult fear laced with adult questions. Inside my head voices asked questions. *Will I be able to handle the training mentally and physically? I'm not military. Will I be able to catch up? For God's sake, I am forty-seven years old!* I screamed in the recesses of my mind. Then guilt engulfed me; guilt and concern for my husband and kids. *How will they manage without me?* My thoughts held no answer.

Spiritually I was a wreck. All my life I had been a devout Catholic. I married in the church, raised my children in the church, attend Mass every week, went to Confession. My yard, the house, all held religious artifacts. I never went anywhere without my rosary and now the Blessed Mother medal that hung around my neck. All were outward demonstrations of my devotion to God and the Catholic way. I truly believed that through my actions and deeds, I had "earned" a good life. Deployment changed all that.

19

God! Why are you doing this to me? Is this my reward? Military deployment is my reward? It was too much to comprehend. I felt like I was being punished for something. But what? I prayed for guidance and understanding. None came.

The Army van that collected me and the other nurses at the airport was silent as we neared the base. We were fourteen women, experienced nurses, most more than thirty, leaving husbands and children at home, wondering what was going to happen to us...wondering if we would be able to handle our situations.

Army barracks turned out to be luxurious compared to what I had imagined. We were housed in an Econo-Lodge, normally reserved for visiting friends and family. The base was bulging with men and women from other reserve units, so troops were being quartered in local motels. I didn't mind a bit.

Grady, the nurse from Lorain, Ohio, was my assigned roommate. We had met briefly at the two reserve drills I had attended back home and had talked during the plane ride to San Antonio. Though we didn't know it then, we were destined to become soul mates for life.

Fort Sam Houston is the medical science center for the Army. Brooks Hospital boasts a famous and impressive burn center among its facilities. We couldn't have been sent to a better place for training.

The next thirteen days were the most learning-intensive I have ever experienced. Our main job was to learn how to command and deal with the possibility and aftermath of nuclear, biological and chemical (NBC) warfare. "It will be your mission," boomed the colonel, "to get the grunts off of the field, put them back together and ship them out!"

The possible consequences of nuclear, biological or chemical (NBC) attacks are terrifying. Nerve gas, phosphorus burns, radiation, mine injuries...terrifying. Each has the potential to inflict extreme suffering and death to a multitude of people at once. Each demands different approaches to care. Each procedure learned tore at our emotions.

To help others survive an NBC attack, you had to first protect yourself. Critical to survival was learning to wear and function in a gas mask and a suit, charcoal lined and rubberized. Timing was a critical factor. In a crisis situation, you had eight seconds to get your mask on and a total of six minutes for your full protective suit. The alert, a loud siren and verbal command, when given, would be called MOPP (Mission Oriented Protective Posture) followed by numbers 1 through 4, depending on the level of readiness required. MOPP I meant suit and jacket, up to MOPP IV which encompassed everything: pants, jacket, over-boots, gas mask and gloves. When MOPP III or MOPP IV was sounded, gas masks went on first. Your survival would depend on how quickly you could get into MOPP readiness. In addition, you had to learn to function suited up...actually do your job. There was no way of telling how long you might be in a state of MOPP IV readiness. It could be hours or days.

Wearing a gas mask proved to be a difficult challenge. The first time I put one on, I panicked. The rubber, smelling like disinfectant, cool and tacky, suctioned in spots to my moist skin. It seemed as if the walls in the room were closing in, crushing me, only I could move my arms and breathe. I felt totally alone, claustrophobic. I ripped it off and looked around breathing hard. No one else seemed as upset. I calmed myself down, took a deep breath and put it on again, this time talking to myself. *Concentrate on the breathing, Dianah....If everyone else can do this, so can you....One breath in....One breath out.... Like swimming underwater, only better....You're not getting wet....Keep it up....You can do it....See....You're doing it!*

Self-talk enabled me to arrange logically the tasks I had to do. It helped control the emotions that were bubbling under the surface, ready to explode. I was able to get a seal right away, which meant that I was breathing properly. Even though the lenses cleared, they were still blurry. My vision is terrible without glasses, and glasses won't fit in a gas mask. Those of us who wore glasses were told that prescription gas mask lenses had been ordered, but there was no way of knowing how long it would take to get them. We would all have to learn how to function in MOPP IV readiness without clear vision.

Wearing a gas mask properly, we were to learn, would not guarantee protection. Total protection came only from encasing every inch of your body in charcoal and rubber. The charcoal lined suits we practiced wearing were unbelievable. Even if it was only 70 degrees outside, the energy in your body would build up and make you sweat terribly. If you sweat, you ran the risk of breaking the seal in your gas mask which would render it useless within a few seconds. Picking up a pencil wearing the thick rubber gloves that completed MOPP IV readiness, was a another challenge; performing simple nursing tasks, next to impossible. I couldn't imagine having to function as a nurse in them. But, still we practiced.

Injuries from traditional weapons were also studied. We learned about potential injuries from grenade and gunfire. The Iraqis might use Soviet made AK-47's, whose bullets twist and turn once they hit their target. The potential for massive internal injuries and traumatic amputations was great.

In addition to medical training, we received intensive weapons training. Even doctors and nurses are expected to be able to defend themselves if the compound is over-run. The M16 rifle, 9 MM handgun, a .45 pistol, and hand grenades were to be mastered. Maneuvering with a compass was also a requirement. Each demanded a certain level of competence. We had 13 days to conquer and qualify on them all.

None of us wanted to know or even think about the possibility of ever having to use any of this training. Yet, we wanted to remember it all. It was important to absorb everything that we could. One thing became very clear; if you didn't survive, the 40 or so injured soldiers in your care wouldn't survive either.

It helped me to intellectualize and rationalize that all this was good basic knowledge, even if I never needed it, so I studied hard and learned all I could. My survival instinct is strong. I was determined to make sure that I would qualify in every way, so that I could save myself and whoever was with me, if need be.

From sunrise to sunset we studied, studied, studied; continuous input all the time. It was worse than any chemistry or microbiology class I had ever taken. There were handouts coming out of our ears. "Take these back to your rooms and go over them for tomorrow," the instructors said after each class. Yeah, right! You took them back to your room with the best of intentions, but by evening, you were so exhausted, that the minute you lay down, you were out.

Marching in formation was part of the training. We drilled each morning at 5:15 A.M. in the Econo Lodge parking lot. The army tried to make us "military minded." It was a difficult task. Doctors and nurses have the mindset that, "this is what I can do for you, you don't have to show me how." The army was determined to teach us to march anyhow.

We were lined up in squads (rows) with a squad leader. Five rows, each row a squad, made up a platoon. This was the first time army drill instructors were being used with reserve medical officers. These drill instructors, enlisted lifers, were accustomed to enlisted men and women. They were rough, gruff and authoritative types who expected immediate compliance. They were faced with physicians and nurses, take-charge people used to giving orders not taking them. Most had been in the army reserves for years but had never gone to OBT. The drill instructors had their hands full.

Teaching us to march was a challenge. You would think that people capable of mastering chemistry and microbiology would be able to tell their right foot from their left, but that is not necessarily so. Our platoon was having so much trouble that one night we asked one of the drill instructors to meet us at 4:00 A.M. the next morning to help us out. Several of us stumbled out into the darkness for this extra training.

"Left face!" came the command. Four of us turned to the right.

"Parade rest!" Three of us kept marching and banged into those in front. We looked like we were auditioning for a Laurel & Hardy movie.

"Attention!" came the order.

"Am I doing this right?" I whispered to Grady.

"Just follow me. Do what I do," she said

The next thing I knew, "Ralph" (drill instructor) put his face up to mine and said, "You're not being a good nurse!"

I looked right at him and shouted back, "How do you know?"

Turning bright red he shouted back, "You're not supposed to talk back because I'm a major and you're just a nurse!"

"Yes, sir!" I responded, seething over his "just a nurse" comment. I wasn't going to let him get to me.

In the middle of another drill, an American-born doctor of Asian descent became disgusted with the whole procedure and walked off the drill site back to his room. He just left.

Stone faced and stoic, the drill instructor continued, his red face glowing in the sunrise...the only hint of his rising frustration. I don't know how he maintained his composure. We surely didn't. Our faces were red too...red from the hysterical laughter we fought to contain. It was apparent that simple maneuvers were beyond our realm of comprehension. We were obviously used to more complicated tasks. Looking for a scapegoat, we blamed our inability to march on the army regulation boots we had to wear. They fit poorly. Our feet would be screaming after a few hours. The boots made it difficult to put one foot in front of the other, let alone march. We stumbled along, like a klutz cluster. Blisters were the badge of the day and Band-Aids became a prized and cherished commodity. Maybe it was because we were army reservists, or maybe it was because we were doctors and nurses, or maybe it was because these were extraordinary circumstances, or maybe it was because we only had 13 days, but we were allowed to get away with such antics. The one thing we were all totally focused, disciplined and united about, however, was learning all we could about the consequences of modern warfare, so that we could do our jobs and accomplish our mission to save as many lives as possible.

Many wonderful people walked into my life in San Antonio. It amazed me how many were in the same position as I...professional men and women who had left jobs, friends and family to serve their country. The median age was well above thirty, although some had just graduated from college. They came from all over the United States: California, Florida, South Carolina, and even Puerto Rico. Like me, the majority had enlisted because of the opportunities available for higher education and a deeply in-grained sense of patriotism. Many names have escaped me. Most faces I will never see again.

People came from all walks of life, from different circumstances. Fascinating people. I remember a nurse from Kentucky who had been commissioned on November 23rd and deployed the very next day. And a plastic surgeon from the Cleveland Clinic kept us in stitches...laughing. He promised me a face lift after this was all over.

Then there was a neurologist from El Paso, Texas, who could hardly walk. He was around sixty years old and had some type of neurological problem with his legs. "Why are you here?" I asked him.

"Because they called me," he replied. He then shared the story of his immigration from Russia to the United States approximately twenty-five years earlier. He went into great detail about how much he would lose by this deployment. "I'll be bankrupt in six months," he said...a reality for most of the doctors who served. He was okay about that. The United

States had afforded him many opportunities. He was very grateful and felt this was the least he could do.

The medical unit of the National Guard in San Juan was there also. Somehow, I became their leader at the pistol range. We were lined up and the captain was going through explanations about the care and use of the pistol...what you do and don't do. It was all fine and dandy except that the San Juan reservists didn't understand a word of what was being said. To say they were having comprehension difficulties was an understatement. "I think we have a problem here, sir," I interjected. "You'd better find someone who can speak Spanish or were in for big trouble." A Spanish speaking recruit was brought in, and the lesson went smoothly from then on.

Most important was Grady, my roommate, my friend, my sanity, my stability, my soul mate. The more we shared, the closer we became. We had so much in common it was spooky: similar life circumstances, husbands, children, jobs. We even had sons already serving in the Persian Gulf. She seemed to understand me and know when to be strong, or emotional, or silly, or intense. The feeling was mutual, and we shared "the good, the bad and the ugly." We kept each other rooted in reality, just enough to make it through, learn all we had to learn, and do what we had to do to survive.

There were 400 people in our class, class #901, all trying to learn everything, absorb everything, praying that this knowledge would never be put to use. Emotions ran high the entire thirteen days. Everyone was afraid. Not knowing what was going to happen to us, wanting yet not really wanting to know, took an emotional toll. Four hundred Reservists were riding a continuous physical and emotional roller coaster. We connected out of desperation, trying to make some sense out of being there; all take-charge individuals, decision makers, suddenly thrown together, for we knew not what. The army brought us together, gave us knowledge and then would send us on our way.

CHAPTER THREE

"He prepares me for battle and gives me strength to draw an iron bow!"

Psalm 18 verse 9

OBT lasted thirteen days, but learning ceased for me on the eleventh day following the General's announcement.

"All of you in this room are going to Saudi Arabia!"

The words shot around the room like a lightning bolt and struck my body full blast! My neck prickled as the hairs began to rise. Dizzy and nauseous at the same time, I grabbed the chair for support. *Breathe! Breathe!* I willed my body to function. Everything reeled in slow motion. My body stiffening, understood long before my mind could accept what my ears had heard. The announcement brought a collective gasp followed by silence...shocked silence. Four hundred pairs of eyes focused on the general as he casually picked up his briefcase, returned the cigar to his pursed lips, scanned the audience one more time, turned and lightly stepped out of the room. Just like that!

For a fraction of a second, after the doors closed, time seemed to stand still. Stunned silence was followed by murmurs, then a roar of disbelief. The tension that had been building for eleven days, exploded in the room. The words, "Saudi Arabia, desert, war" could be heard in various forms echoing throughout the hall.

Frantically, I turned to those on either side of me and began to babble. "Wait a minute! Wait just a minute. We're all doctors and nurses, and our job is in the United States...the military hospitals in the United States. That's what the recruiter said. 'Army Reservists would not be deployed outside of the United States.' Those were his exact words!" My mind raced in all directions teetering between logic and emotion, rational fighting the irrational, trying to get a grip on it; trying to comprehend what we had just been told.

Before I knew it, Grady was by my side, and we were both talking at the same time. "Hey, this way we'll be close to our sons!" she joked hysterically.

"Now that's looking on the bright side," I said hugging her through my tears.

Within minutes, maybe seconds, we were joined by three others...nurses from the Toledo reserves. All around us small groups were coming together; mini-communities, pockets of emotional strength. Some sat stoic, alone, trying to understand what they had been told. But most had turned toward their brothers and sisters in the military for strength and support. The strength of the camaraderie that had been building during the last eleven days was never more evident. It would be this support, the support of fellow soldiers, and a belief in a Higher Power that would get me through the next months.

I am sure that dyed-in-the-wool enlisted military types would have been appalled at our behavior. Visions of well-disciplined troops come to mind, accepting the inevitable with a crisp salute and bravery, daring not to show emotions or question lest reprimands occur. The Army Reserve Medical Units were not that disciplined or that accepting. We were highly trained professional men and women used to taking charge, order-makers not order-takers.

Following the general's exit, we were called back to order. A brief question and answer period was allowed. "Has the U.S. declared war?" No. "Why are we going?" "Where are we going?" "When are we going?" everyone wanted to know. "What is America's status over there right now?" Most of the questions couldn't be or wouldn't be answered for security reasons. We were beginning to understand just how the military machine really operated. Orders are given. Questions are answered, in due time...army time. One didn't have to be too discerning to figure out that our country was headed for war and that we were going to be in the thick of it.

The intensive training all made sense, now. Intellectually, I guess I knew it all along, but before the announcement, I couldn't let myself believe it. A little more than two months earlier, I had been a middle-class housewife, mother, grandmother and nurse, content with life, but interested in college. Now, I was being ordered into the desert and a possible war. It was too frightening to contemplate.

I wasn't alone in my feelings. Many of my comrades felt the same way. Outside critics might think we were acting like spoiled kids. Perhaps to some degree we were. But, like children whose parents give them everything, it wasn't our fault. Many of the doctors and nurses who had been in the reserves for years never had been sent to OBT nor had any semblance of military discipline at their monthly drills. They had come to accept a relaxed military that allowed for their input.

Whiners!..You knew what the risks were, others criticized. I don't think most did. Mobilization and action in a war zone are expected when you enlist in the regular army, but the doctors and nurses who had enlisted in the army reserves, almost without exception, had been told that if mobilized in wartime, they would never be used in a war theater. Duty, if at all, would be a state-side assignment or a support hospital in a neutral country.

The information that we had been given was false. The real truth of the matter was, that in a military crisis situation, the majority of the medical corps would come from reserve units.

Why had I been so gullible when signing up? I asked myself. I should have been more discerning when I spoke to the recruiter. Yes, he did tell me that an Evac Hospital was a field hospital set up near the front lines to stabilize and evacuate the injured from the Combat Support Hospitals (CSH) and the MASH units. So, in that sense, I knew exactly what I had signed up for. But, he also made a big point of emphasizing the fact that the reserve units would never be sent into a war zone. Our orders were unexpected and many in the Reserve Medical Units felt betrayed by the lack of information they had originally been given; things conveniently left unsaid. Serving in the most forward evacuation hospital in a war zone was certainly not one of my expectations. Would I have signed up if I had known? I can't honestly say.

Class resumed, but concentration was next to impossible, even though we now knew that it was essential to remember every detail. The focus of the class was on map reading. I remember something about shooting the isthmus off a compass...how difficult it would be without an object to shoot it off of and how you could make it work in the desert. Important stuff to remember. Critical for survival. My brain wouldn't focus. All I could think of was, *you're going to Saudi Arabia! You're going to the desert! Deal with it!* Like a broken record the words played over and over in my head, preparing me for acceptance of all that was to come.

We were sent home for three days following OBT, but not for rest and relaxation. The minute we arrived we were ordered to Canton, Ohio, our home base, for inventory duty. Everyone was really pissed-off. We had expected to have this time with our families, but no, we had to work. It was the first time I fully realized that the army now called the shots. I was active duty and had no choice but to comply.

The news media must have psychic powers because they were at my house within fifteen minutes after my arrival. In the middle of my interview with them, my daughter, Mary, arrived home from school and their TV cameras recorded our emotional reunion.

Wanting to appear brave and together, I demonstrated the use of the gas mask for the media and my family. Putting it on within eight seconds, in the middle of my living room, in front of my family, was emotionally devastating. I started to panic and ripped it off, upset. I had meant to waylay their fears with my competence, but instead tapped into my thin mask of bravery. It was an emotional struggle to keep my composure.

Telling Tom and the children of my orders was extremely difficult, but they took it quite well. "The desert, after all, is a big place," I laughed, pretending confidence. I assured them that I wasn't crazy or afraid about it. Upset? Yes, but not afraid. I was a well-trained nurse and prepared to do the job for my country. Somehow my words sounded confident, camouflaging the terror in my heart...at least from them.

Sunday, our day off, I tried to absorb all the normal life I could. Walking from room to room, I memorized every wall in the house, every object, every texture and smell, everything that was home to me. We went to Mass, but I don't remember much about it: I just went through the motions: It didn't comfort me as before. I felt betrayed and alone. For the first time, I was questioning God's place in my life, my faith had been shattered.

My emotions were fragile at best. I was numb and moved as if in another dimension; there, yet not really there. I loved my family so much and wanted to be supportive for them, but every second was a fight to keep in control. I knew that I was prepared to do my job, but what about them? My husband? My family? Would they be able to cope with this? What about Mary and her senior year in high school? What if Tom had a heart attack? What about Dave already in the Persian Gulf? What if his ship was hit? How would I deal with that? The "what ifs?"...things that I couldn't do anything about, were overwhelming. So much to say. So much to do. I had to make every moment count.

The buses pulled out of Canton, Ohio, very early the next morning, bound for Fort Benjamin Harrison, in Indiana. Everyone was quiet, lost in thoughts of things said, things left unsaid and what the future could bring.

Our bus driver, a soldier "wannabe," made up for our silence. We heard his life story all the way to Indianapolis. "I want to join the Marines, and go over and kill some Iraqis," he said. Although annoying to an extent, he did make us laugh. He even serenaded us with a Marine song he had learned from some buddies. He was really proud to be part of this war effort and driving us to Fort Ben.

"These guys are going to Saudi, give them a toot!" he shouted into his CB radio to truckers passing by. The resulting blast on their horns made us all feel proud. Some truckers even relayed their military stories. They all were encouraging.

This was our first taste of the tremendous support that was to come from the American people. My brother is a trucker, so I know what a tough job it is. Each response made me feel closer to him.

I could never sleep in moving cars, trains or buses. Some can, but not I. I was filled with tension and anxiety over what was to come.

Fort Benjamin Harrison, lived up to its reputation: an infamous hole-in-the-wall, a dive. We were grouped and moved into rooms of nine; nine women and one bathroom, cot to cot to cot to cot. Sharing such close quarters with friends would have been difficult, let alone nine strangers, of all ages, with different family circumstances, moral values, religions and lifestyles.

I'd always prided myself on being able to get along with almost everyone, and I did, with seven of the eight in my room. One gal, however, drove me up the wall! She was about twenty six, going on fifteen. Moody, arrogant, pouty, childish and rude. She had "Gibraltar" on her shoulder, an arrogance that exuded an "operating room nurses are better than you are" attitude. For awhile, I chalked my sensitivity to her up to being nervous and scared, but she was downright mean at times. We all had quirks which were exaggerated because of the unusual circumstances we found ourselves in. I had been through this kind of adolescent behavior with my five kids, and I wasn't about to go through it again with a stranger. The day I found her in a drunken stupor, retching on the bathroom floor, was the last straw. I packed my things and moved out!

Hosslern and Wagner, friends from OBT, weren't happy with their roommate situation, either. Together, the three of us, without authorization, left our rooms and moved in with Grady. Her room was crowded, but at least we were with people who shared similar backgrounds, morals, attitudes and thought processes. It made living so much easier. We didn't have to deal with someone getting drunk and puking on the floor. It was great.

Classes at Fort Ben. were a recap of OBT. Only this time, we knew for sure where we were headed. The pressure to perfect our skills was immense. We wanted to make absolutely certain that we understood everything.

NBC training, though no less terrifying, seemed easier. Familiarity with basic procedures for handling the consequences, allowed us to focus on what we didn't know. I felt comfortable asking in-depth questions. Before, I didn't even know what questions I should be asking.

Protective dress procedures, in the event of an NBC attack, were emphasized repeatedly. Into the gas mask and charcoal suit and out again, we practiced. It was still challenging. "Your life and the lives of your patients will depend on your being able to do this." carried more meaning now that we knew where we were going.

Getting into a MOPP IV suit in the allotted time was a battle. Working in one was the ultimate challenge. Thick rubber gloves, limited vision through gas mask goggles, thick rubber boots and cumbersome jackets made performing simple medical procedures almost impossible. We had to practice them anyway. Practice, practice, practice. In the event of an attack, we would need to keep working. We were grilled and drilled on techniques for specific kinds of wounds: chest, the need for amputations, burns, all the predictable consequences of the use of modern-day weaponry. A learning center contained audio and video tapes to reinforce much of the training. I found it particularly helpful when I was trying to learn the different armaments, helicopters, tanks, airplanes, and other land vehicles. We all had to be able to discern who was coming down the road or flying overhead. Weapons training started all over again. Even though I had already qualified on the M-16 rifle, the 9 MM hand gun, .45 pistol, and hand grenades, down in Texas, I had to do it again. This time veterans from Vietnam and other wars did the training. They were very thorough and serious about their jobs. Each and every one of us would be well-trained and proficient in the use of all of these firearms before being shipped out.

It had been raining the day that I re-qualified on the M-16, and mud was everywhere. Curtis, a young African-American from Cleveland, was helping me. Check and double check. I helped him. He helped me. I was a challenge for him because I am left-handed, and the cartridges kept hitting me in the head. He hung in patiently. We were both covered with mud by the end of the session. That's the way it was: male, female, white, black, yellow...soldier helping soldier. If you didn't, you would have a tough time. The days were physically and emotionally draining, much worse than in OBT. Like OBT, in the evening, back in the room, exhaustion invariably crept in and ruined planned study sessions. During the day I was kept so busy that I had very little time to react emotionally to all that I was learning or even think about home. But often, in the quiet of my bed, reaction would engulf me.

My faith had wavered after receiving my mobilization orders in November, so much so that morning and evening prayers, once so comforting, now meant nothing to me. I rattled them off from memory and habit. But now there was always the question, *why me, God? What am I doing here?*

No answer came. I struggled to understand why God would send me, a forty-seven year old grandmother into a potential war zone. I had always been a spiritual person and believed that God had a purpose for my life, but since being deployed, things were no longer clear. I felt abandoned. Was my faith...had my faith been only superficial? I'd followed all the rules. Lived all the rituals. Is that all it was...a lifetime of going through the motions? I was confused, lost, afraid as never before, like Peter in the fishing boat in the storm questioning Jesus who had commanded him to walk on water. Sinking, Peter cried out, "Lord save me!" Stretching out his hand catching Peter, the Lord said, "Oh you of little faith, why did you doubt?" *Was that the answer? Was my faith too little? Was I doubting too much?*

Although Grady hadn't known me long, she recognized that something about me had changed. I was more tense, more angry, less able to put up with the rigors of daily life. When weekend Mass was announced and I refused to go, she knew the problem was something major.

"C'mon Kwiatkowski, time for Mass!" she announced matter-of-factly.

"Go ahead," I said. "I'm not interested."

"What'd you mean, not interested? You're the most religious person here."

"I don't think so," I offered sadly.

"Cut the crap, Kwiatkowski. You're going. Now get dressed! That's an order!" she shouted.

I glared at her, angry that she would dare to impose something as personal as religion on me like that.

"Don't give me that look," she said, standing her ground. "You don't have to listen, but you are going if I have to get Hosslern and Wagner to help drag you!"

I wasn't angry at her, of course. I was angry at the God I thought had abandoned me. Reluctantly, I followed her to Mass.

Mass was held in a multi-purpose chapel used for services by all faiths. It was tiny. Father Joe, the priest, was a small man, dark hair, very charismatic, very open, loving and focused on the troops. He made me mad. I wasn't ready to accept loving words. With every assurance, my mind screamed, *if God cares so much, why is he sending me to Saudi Arabia?*

As if sensing my mental anguish, reading my pain he preached, "Do not question God's plan for you. Accept it with joy...the joy of knowing that He loves you and prepares a place for you. For every day there is a season and a plan under heaven."

Following Mass, I was a wreck. Outwardly, I stubbornly pretended indifference. Deep down, I had to admit that Mass was wonderful. I felt as though the message was written especially for me. Even so, I was still too angry at God to give in. Father Joe grabbed my hand as we walked out. I stiffened at his touch. He held firm, his hands warm and strong. "Lieutenant Kwiatkowski," he said, "God has a plan for you. I know you can't see it now, but he needs your skills in the desert. He will be with you. All things will become clear in due time. Be patient, my dear."

His words cut through what little resolve I had left. I wrenched my hand from his and ran back to the barracks, sobbing. He knew my name. He knew who I was, I marveled.

Later, in a calm, more composed state, I realized that he had read my name plate.

Father Joe, in his quiet way, did break through my resolve. I began attending Mass, again, as often as I could. Guarded, yet open to his message, I struggled to believe as I had before; trust the way I had before. All the while I knew that my faith would never be the same.

Morning and evening prayers continued, although with less fervor. Like a well-programmed machine, I rattled off memorized prayers. No longer was I having personal conversations with the Lord. The words wouldn't come. So, I meditated. It was during one of my meditations that I started to think about the prayers to Saint Michael the Archangel and all his angels, God's warriors and the protector of warriors. The last time I had thought about them was as a child, when we had studied about them in CCD class. I remember being fascinated that God had angels to protect warriors. Why I should think of them now was a mystery. I became obsessed with the prayers. I knew I had to have them to take with me. The next time I went to Mass, I lingered after the service and cornered Father Joe.

"Father Joe, I really need to have the prayers of Saint Michael. Do you have a prayer card with them on it? The prayer goes something like, 'Saint Michael the Archangel, defend us in battle. Be our protector against...' I can't remember it all. I just know I have to have them."

Father Joe's eyes brightened with delight. "Yes, yes, of course, Saint Michael. Wise choice Kwiatkowski. I'd forgotten about Saint Michael. Come with me. I'm sure I have copies in my office."

"The church in my town has not been big on Saint Michael for awhile," I said as we walked toward his office. "I don't know why. The priest we had several years ago said the prayers before each Mass 'to rid the church of any satanic influence or evil spirits,' he used to say."

"Well, you know, Dianah, there are trends in the church too. We priests are human after all," he laughed holding the office door open for me. Following me through, he unzipped his vestment and hung it up in the closet. "Sit down, Lieutenant Kwiatkowski," he said motioning to a chair near his desk. "This should only take a minute."

"Let's see," he said to himself thumbing through the file drawer, "prayer cards, Humm!" He pulled out several pamphlets banded together with rubber bands. "Nope, not there." He closed the drawer and opened the next one down. "Saint Michael. Saint Michael. Aha!, Saint Michael, here it is." He pulled a file folder out and began to look. Inside was a sermon he had preached, but none of the prayers was included. "Now where are they?" he asked himself. He turned to his desk and rifled through the drawers and then walked over to his closet. "They've got to be here," he kept saying. Perspiration beaded up on his forehead as he continued to look. I could tell he was getting frustrated. Finally, he turned to me, defeated.

"I'm really sorry, Lieutenant Kwiatkowski, I can't find them. I don't know where they are! The prayers of Saint Michael are wonderful...a wise choice for your mission. They would be helpful in the desert. Thank you for reminding me of them. I'll keep looking, and I'll let you know if I find them before you leave. I'm sorry, so sorry."

"That's okay, Father Joe," I said trying not to sound too disappointed. Of course I was...very.

Father Joe opened one last drawer. "Aha!" he said confidently. I looked up excited. He pulled a calendar out of the drawer and pushed it across the desk in my direction.

"Here, Kwiatkowski," he said.

"The prayers?" I said hopeful.

"No, not the prayers. But, this might help,." he said, hopeful.

"A calendar?" I asked questioning.

"I call it my all-Saints calendar," he responded, joyfully. "Take it and use it to keep a mini-journal of events. A word, a sound, an expression. Write something each day. Something to trigger memories of events you live through. Memories of the proof of God's grace. Each day a different one selected by God to bring you a daily reminder of His presence. Pray to the Saints, Lieutenant Kwiatkowski. They'll help you." Father Joe could see I was disappointed about the prayers. Before I could say anything he continued. "Oh," he said, "one more thing." He reached into another drawer and pulled out a small box. Opening it he pulled out a beautiful Celtic Cross, on a chain. "You missed the Mass where we handed these out," he said as he carefully placed it over my head. It fell around my neck joining the Blessed Mother medal that for years had held so much meaning.

Disappointed, I choked back tears, thanked him for the calendar and the cross, and hurried out of the office.

We were sent home for five days at Christmas time. It was wonderful being back in my own home, in my own bed, with my own family, doing the things that up until a few weeks prior, had been my daily routine. Sights, sounds, smells... everything so familiar had suddenly taken on greater significance. I cherished every moment.

Throughout my house the religious symbols of what my faith used to be, beckoned. The hanging crosses, the pictures, Saint Teresa at the foot of the stairs, the head of Christ in the family room. *Trust...believe...I have not left you,* they seemed to say. I wanted to feel as I had. But, my faith had changed...was still changing.

My friend, Betty, gathered some friends for a Hello Goodbye party. It was great seeing everyone. I took pictures and laughed to keep from crying. It was really hard. Everyone was acting relaxed, "normal" about everything. Yet we were all thinking, *maybe we'll never see each other again.*

Several friends questioned me about my training and the political issues surrounding the Middle East situation. I tried not to get too political. Even so, I had many discussions about the war being an "oil" issue, an economic issue. I believed it was more of a human-rights issue. All I really cared about was that my mission was to protect and help American and allied troops through my gift of trauma nursing. And this I had vowed to do to the best of my ability.

Once again, the media invaded my privacy. Although they were a great intrusion into my personal life, I felt an obligation to let moms and dads know that there would be mature people over in the Gulf, taking care of their sons and daughters. I wanted to let people know that the personnel in the medical corps were all experienced and if there was any way to keep someone alive, there wasn't any doubt in my mind that we would find that way.

"How does it feel to be home at Christmas?" asked the reporter. "Blessed!" I responded. "Blessed with a loving family and friends. And, blessed to live in this great country of ours. Make no mistake, I was shocked when my orders came. But, when you take an oath and are commissioned, you are taking an oath to serve. You vow to support the constitution, and guard against foreign aggression."

The support group met while I was home, so I stopped by for one last visit. People were devastated that I had been called up. My role in the group had completely reversed. I tried hard to get them to understand that I would be taking care of their kids, their loved ones and that they would be okay.

"Dianah...why are we there?" asked a gentleman whose son was deployed. "This conflict. This oil thing?"

"It's not a conflict, it's an invasion...let's keep that straight!" I told them. "Prior to being mobilized, I couldn't have told you much about Kuwait. I thought it was family owned, a monarchy. I wasn't sure if it had a constitution. That really doesn't matter. What matters is that Iraq has invaded and is robbing the country blind." Everyone listened intently to my every word. I got up and began to pace. "I keep thinking about my oldest son's college roommate, Mark, and his family. He was a young man from Kuwait. A great kid. He spent many weekends in my home. I keep wondering if he and his family are okay. They represent all of the people of Kuwait to me. Knowing that I'm going to help them has helped me adjust to my orders."

Christmas. The whole family got together at my sister-in-law's house. She went all-out with food and other little touches to make sure that this Christmas would be perfect for me. It was a magical day. Stories of past Christmases and other family memories charged us all with laughter and tears. Though, midst the joy and laughter, was an air of expectancy...the feeling that perhaps we would never again all be together. Everyone felt it. I kept pushing it to the back of my mind. Nothing was going to spoil my last day home. Besides, I couldn't even comprehend the family not being together like this ever again. Perhaps it was my arrogance or the total focus of attention on what I was about to do that it never occurred to any of us that that feeling would explode into reality so soon, but not because of me.

The difficult thing about being home was having to say, "good-bye" again. This time it was especially hard, since I knew and they knew, I was being sent out of the country for an indefinite period of time. Everyone tried to be light and humorous about everything. Smiling was hard.

In just a month, I noticed a big change within myself and my relationship with both my family and friends. None of them could relate to what I had been through and what I would be going through. It was the feeling you get after a great vacation when you try to share your experiences. You know that unless others have been there too, no one will be able to relive your trip.

December 26th we Reservists said our last good-byes and boarded buses bound for Fort Ben. For nine days we were run through the ropes...yet again. It was a total rehash of Officer Basic and the last 14 days we had spent there. For the third time, we had to qualify on all of the weapons. It seemed like mismanagement of time, time that would have been better spent working within our platoons, checking levels of experience and expertise and finding out what our unit's strengths and weaknesses were.

On December 27th, news arrived that my sister-in-law had passed away. My dear sister-in-law who had given my whole family the best Christmas ever just two days earlier. It was not to be believed! Her death shattered my already shaky emotions.

I immediately applied for a 24-hour release to attend the funeral, but my request was denied. Sister-in-laws are not considered immediate family. Words cannot describe how angry I was. My husband was extremely close to his sister, and I knew that he needed me. It hurt me knowing that he had to go through this by himself. I was beside myself with grief. My sisters in the military tried to help, but it was prayer that got me through: Prayer, mechanical, angry and bitter at first; prayer that changed somewhere in the midst of the words...prayer that comforts. My sister-in-law was very spiritual. Prayer helped me feel close to her.

New Year's Eve came and we were determined to make the best of it. Several of us got together and had a little party. We tried to be joyful. We focused our attention on each other to keep our minds off of what we were missing back home. Each person had his or her own story.

There was McCracken, a LPN from a Midwestern town. His wife was pregnant and having a rough time physically and emotionally. He tried to get out of going to Saudi, but he had to go anyway. At first we felt sorry for him. Later, when he pulled some strings and got sent home, we were really furious.

Schaffer was a very determined, gutsy gal; a single mom who refused to turn custody of her son over to her ex-husband.

Instead, she brought him (her son) with her. She was trying to work it out with the military to take care of him. This four-year-old was amid hundreds of military personnel being prepared for a potential war. I don't know how Schaffer did it, but she did. Her strategy paid off. She managed to get re-assigned to an Army hospital in Virginia, where they apparently needed an anesthetist. She was lucky.

Grady, Hosslern, Allargo, Vanderwal, Warner and Wagner, friends from OBT, were there also. We shared personal stories, tried to laugh and act upbeat. But, it was very sad. How do you toast a New Year that was propelling you into the middle of a potential war zone? How do you toast a New Year that you may never experience fully? How do you toast a New Year in which you may never again see your family? This dilemma united us with hundreds of thousands of other military personnel attempting to do the same thing. New Year's Eve was a difficult evening.

The next several days, in addition to re-hashing all that we had learned in OBT, moved us through a maze of paperwork and other necessary procedures that had to be completed. Hours were wasted sitting on chairs and waiting in lines to sign papers or have pictures taken. Units were being deployed from all over the country at the same time. One unit might be lined up at point C geometrically, another at A, and another at B or D. It was extremely confusing. You were never sure if you were in the right place, or the right line doing the right thing at the right time.

The enlisted office personnel weren't much help, even though it was their responsibility to activate and direct us from area to area. They were rude and clueless. You could sit for two days in a chair, and no one would question why you were there or offer to help you.

One day, Grady and I were waiting on the lower level of a three story building to process our Geneva Conventions pictures. The Geneva Conventions, starting back in 1864, provide for the humane treatment of prisoners of war and the wounded during wartime. It also provides for the protection of civilians and militia and volunteer corps, such as the Red Cross. Each military person was given a special card with specific personal information on it including a picture, to wear in case of capture and a reminder to the enemy of the regulations set forth and agreed upon at the Geneva Conventions. Ironically, Iraq does not honor the Geneva Convention.

Anyway, Grady and I were are waiting for our pictures, when suddenly, a young enlisted army personnel office worker came bouncing down the stairs laughing and talking loudly.

"I can't believe how stupid some of these reservists are!" she proclaimed. "They can't seem to follow simple directions! You won't believe what this one guy upstairs asked?" She lowered her head, closer to her co-worker, out of ear shot, and continued to mumble something. Soon they were both howling.

I could feel my blood pressure rising. *Who does she think she is?* I thought. One glance at Grady told me she was thinking the same thing.

Presently, the howling duo were joined by an NCO, (non-commissioned officer) who was apparently their boss. I am not sure what rank he was. I think he was a First Sergeant. Once again we listened to the tale of our own stupidity, followed this time by his booming laughter. *Well you jerk!* I thought. He should have known better. His years of experi ence should have told him that these people, these reservists, were under extreme stress. Sure they asked stupid questions, but so what? When you've been thrown into such an inappropriate situation, what's wrong with inappropriate questions?

Up until that moment, I had never exercised my authority as a lieutenant in the military. But, the second telling of the tale plus the movement of the sergeant's stripes as he shook with laughter, drove me to action. My chair creaked as I slid out of it and silently marched across the room. My face must have been red and my ears burning off, because this guy took one look at me and backed away from the desk. "Sergeant!" I shouted as I neared the counter.

"Yes, ma'am!" he responded, snapping to attention.

"I couldn't help but overhear your little conversation, and I'm not amused." The giddy office workers, now wide-eyed also assumed the pose. My words wielded their effect. All heads in the waiting room turned in my direction. "Don't you ever make fun of any reservist again!" I boomed. "I don't care whether they're going to Texas or Germany or Saudi Arabia...they're the ones who are going, while you and your staff will be sitting behind your little desks pushing pencils!" All three jumped as I banged my fist on the desk. "Do you understand what I'm saying?"

"Yes ma'am!" they shouted.

Stepping closer to the First Sergeant, I lowered my voice and continued, "You know, Sergeant, I don't like to use my rank, but I will and I'll take your butt down the tunnel, if I have to! There's no excuse for what I just witnessed. You are the officer here. Start acting like one!"

It was very obvious, by his reaction, that this guy thought that I was capable of taking out my pistol and blowing his balls off! At that very moment, he may have been right. Here we were trying to merge together to form a strong military unit, and this so-and-so was poking fun at us!

I turned, triumphant, filled for the first time with the realization of the power of my rank, and strolled back to the chair in the waiting area. Grady didn't say a thing. She just smiled appreciatively, as did the others who were waiting.

A few days later, Grady and I were back in the same building, sitting in the same chairs, waiting to pick up our new revised "dog tags," when another incident happened. A thunderous noise drew our attention to the stairway where another reservist came bounding down the stairs, obviously agitated. We couldn't tell what rank he was; his fatigues were missing the usual tell-tale badges. Reaching the landing, he walked directly towards the chairs where we were sitting. He started to sit down, changed his mind and began pacing back and forth, back and forth, flexing his fingers, cracking his knuckles and wringing his hands.

"Hi! I'm Lieutenant. Kwiatkowski and this is Lieutenant Grady," I offered hoping to distract him and calm him down a little.

He stopped cracking his knuckles long enough to nod, "Hello."

"Where're you from, soldier?" asked Grady.

"Cleveland...Cleveland, Ohio," he said nervously.

"No kidding!" we both responded in unison.

He perked up a little. "Why, where're you from?" he asked.

"We're from Cleveland, too!" I offered. I'm a nurse in I.C.U. at Southwest General, and Grady works in Lorain. Small world."

"Yeah, small world," he replied. Flopping down in a nearby vacant chair, he began talking, quietly, slowly, at first. "I am a doctor, a surgeon." His foot rhythmically tapped the rung on the chair as he continued cautiously. "I...I am Syrian." Grady and I sat listening attentively. He paused again, as if gauging our possible reaction to his next words. Then, appearing satisfied, the words tumbled out. "My cousins are in the Iraqi Army. How can I go to war against my own family?" he asked tearfully, but more for the telling, not really expecting an answer. "I feel like I can't do this. I can't do this," he repeated. He jumped up and started pacing again. "My wife says I must do this. She says I am an American citizen and a part of the army reserves and I really don't have a choice, unless I want to go to Leavenworth."

"She's right, you know," offered Grady.

"I know, I know, but I just don't think I can do this. I feel so weak inside. I can't do this, and I can't do that. I can't make any decisions. I mean, I want to kill myself."

Grady and I exchange glances of alarm. This young man was really on the edge. Instinctively we knew we must keep him talking. It was our best defense...our best shot at diffusing the situation.

"Your wife is right," I offered, "you wouldn't want to go the prison, now...would you?" He didn't answer.

Absorbed in his own thoughts, he suddenly retorted, "I can speak Arabic fluently."

"That's terrific!" we echoed. "You will be a tremendous asset to your unit. Why, just think of the positive impact you will have on the Arabic people because you can speak to them and we can't."

We talked as long as we could, until our names were called. By that time, Grady and I felt fairly confident that he was going to be okay, at least for that day. I made a pact to meet him that evening on the porch outside of my building. No smoking was allowed inside any of the buildings, so smokers congregated on the porches at night. That evening, sure enough, he was there. I was relieved. He became one of my smoking buddies.

The next several days we were run through more training, more paper work, more lines, more waiting, more questions, fewer answers. The daily routine, the rumors, the expectations, the stress was wearing everyone down. *Will this be the day?* was the question on everyone's mind.

On January 4th, we were brought into formation and told that we would be going deep into the desert. "Be ready!" were the orders. Everything was blacked out! No phone calls were allowed, no contact with family. That was okay. You didn't really want to say good-bye, again. It was too painful.

Buses transported us to Wright Patterson Air Force Base in Dayton, Ohio, where we were locked in with military police.

All around me comrades slept sprawled, crunched, confined on the floor in the rooms we were herded into to await our "chariot" to the desert. Exhausted as I was, I couldn't sleep. Tension and fear, emotional fear, kept me alert.

Across the room a sergeant nodded against her M-16. I fumed. Those few who were issued weapons, even though unloaded, were to assume a ready, responsible posture. She was not following orders.

Stepping carefully over sleeping bodies, I made my way to her side. Reaching out I grabbed the rifle. She jumped to attention muttering, "What the h....?"

Ignoring her comment I said, "You are expected to stay awake when assigned this weapon."

She nodded, furious with the interruption. No words left her lips, but her eyes spoke volumes. *What's the big deal? We're in lock-in for God's sake. Lighten up,* they seemed to say.

"You could lose your rifle and a lot more with that behavior," I chastised, still upset. Again, she stared. Handing the M-16 back to her, I turned and made my way back to my space on the linoleum to wait. At 0400 final orders came. "Line up, two by two. No talking! No questions!" Who could talk? We were too scared! Silently we filed onto the runway and into an unmarked, all white 747.

CHAPTER FOUR

"Why does the Lord bring us into this land, to fall by the sword?"

Numbers 14 verse 3

The airplane door opened onto a world of darkness. Sand, sweat, canvas, metal, jet fuel, fear: smells familiar yet foreign. The damp smell of the desert. And the sounds of hundreds of arriving troops.

The moment my foot hit the sand I was overwhelmed by a sense of evil coursing through my body and piercing my soul as surely as if I had suffered a physical assault. I stumbled under the weight of my backpack, clutching for, yet unable to reach the Blessed Mother medal and cross hanging around my neck. Were it not for the ordered silence, I would have cried out in fear. Momentarily forgetting my anger with God, I began to pray silently.

Jesus, Mary and Joseph, Mother of God, be with me in this heathen land. Help me! Help me! Praise ye Jesus, I give You glory! Saint Michael the Archangel, defend me in battle. Be my protector...my protection...my? Damn, why can't I remember that prayer? I need those prayers! I must get them! Oh, God, why am I here? My mind ran asking questions, searching for answers, something, anything to quell the mounting terror.

The flight to Saudi Arabia had taken sixteen and a half hours during which time I might have slept at most 45 minutes. After a refueling stop in Brussels, Belgium, we finally arrived at King Faud airport, just outside Dhaharan, Saudi Arabia. Dhaharan is a port city on the coast of the Persian Gulf, the main avenue for flow of troops and supplies.

Still before dawn, the sun was just beginning to rise as we marched off the plane single file, into nothingness...no runway lights, no buildings, no trees, no other living things. Just sand, sand and more sand, everywhere.

My God! This looks like a crater on the moon. This has to be a dream. It's not real. I'm not really here. I kicked sand hoping to feel the sheet in my bed back home. Instead, sand sprayed the army boot in front of me. The soldier turned annoyed. I mouthed, "sorry."

It was winter in the desert. The temperature was a cold 40 degrees—much colder than any of us expected. We would soon learn how diverse desert weather could be.

We were not the only unit to disembark that daybreak. Several other groups had also landed. As we were marched by a troop of Marines, we could hear comments, cat calls, growls and sniffs. "Hey, pretty baby!" "Ooohhh, I like!" "I'd sure like to climb into that backpack of yours!" Some of the comments would have made a rattlesnake blush. It was probably just a "guy thing," but, we were tired, frightened, emotionally drained and not in a humorous mood. Whatever their reason, we weren't about to tolerate it. Ordered not to speak, we resorted to the only gesture of power we could think of. It was instinctive. First one, then another, then all of us flipped them off!

Lord, forgive me! Only minutes in the desert and here I am, a mother, grandmother, nurse and a Christian too, giving a group of guys the finger.

Five open-air buses, with curtains on the windows, awaited our unit. Under other circumstances, they were a tourist's photographic dream...quaint, rustic, picturesque. Sand crunched under our boots as we climbed aboard.

The bus driver possessed a mysterious quality. His dark hair and dark darting eyes made me uncomfortable. He didn't speak English, at least not to us. I had the feeling that he understood, but he didn't talk to us, and no one even tried to talk to him. We all had to trust he was on our side and that he knew where we were supposed to go. Many on our bus fell asleep, but I couldn't. I wanted to see where I was being taken.

Our destination, first home, was in Kobar, about three miles outside of Dhaharan. We were driven towards row upon row of condos stacked up like apartments with concertina wire all around them for protection. Kobar Towers was the name of the surprisingly modern complex, which had been built for the Bedouins, nomadic desert people who don't like city living. Consequently, the entire complex was unoccupied for years. Now, it served as a perfect stop-off for organizing troops.

The bus we were on wandered around and around the complex for what seemed like hours, finally coming to rest in one of the many underground parking garages. There we unloaded and were directed to another apartment garage to pick up our duffel bags and trunks. Until room assignments could be made, we were ordered to roll out our sleeping bags on the garage floor. No one minded. We were so exhausted, we all passed out. Later that day, we were moved into one of the buildings.

The apartments were actually nice. Fifty women shared a five bedroom, three bathroom wing. Assignments were made according to rank. Officers together and enlisted together. We got along amazingly well, considering the circumstances.

Our first and biggest problem was water. We had none. The water supply to the women's apartments mysteriously stopped working shortly after we moved in. Since my apartment was on the third floor, it was a real nuisance. But, we made the best of it. We organized into teams, and each day hauled water up the three flights.

Conservation was the name of the game. We became rather resourceful. Showers were out of the question, so we took sponge baths. No one was allowed to flush the toilet unless several had used it first. This was hard for fastidious, bacteria conscious, sanitation obsessed nurses to do...but we did it. We had no choice.

Funny things happened on the way to conservation. One night, in the middle of the night, I got up and had a bowel movement. Not wanting to waste the water or let it sit over night, I woke Marlene up and asked her if she had to go. She nodded, "Yes," got up and did it. So, we shared the water. Later, we laughed and laughed about it. I had awakened her out of a dead sleep. She had "pooped" on command and hardly remembered it. We were furious when we learned later that the water problem was limited to the women's condo only. The problem was not the plumbing at all, it was societal. Arab women, all women, are deemed unworthy of such a luxury. The Arabs did not want female military personnel serving during this crisis. They invoked their "fair" female standards on us. We were furious to learn of this slight, and powerless to do anything about it.

The lack of status for women in Arab cultures is often attributed to the Muslim faith when in fact, it is more of a cultural phenomenon. It began generations ago when the desert tribes fought for land. To ensure loyalty among the conquered desert tribesmen, the leaders would marry their women, and have many wives at one time producing sons for them. Those women were, and women are today, dominated and controlled by the men. Slaves, chattel for men to use and abuse as they wished. A man's pride and public honor are measured by his ability to control his women and beget sons. Daughters are not acknowledged.

Reading about the lowly status of women and experiencing it are two vastly different matters. In our naivete, we figured that we would be exempt. After all, they had sent for us. But, here we were, female American military personnel, doctors and nurses, sent to the desert to help protect and minister to their injured, and we had no rights. Furthermore, we had to put up with harassment.

The water incident, was just a first indication of our lowly status. All women were housed in separate apartment buildings and were threatened with arrest if they dared to enter one of the buildings occupied by men. Nurses were spit upon. One day, an OR (operating room) nurse was walking past a building with several other nurses, when all of a sudden a sand bag landed at her feet, missing her by inches. She could hear laughing and jeering coming from the rooftop. Looking up, she saw the unmistakable blue uniform of the locals. There is no doubt that she would have been killed had she been hit. We all had to be so careful. To be without water was difficult, but not as bad as the sewer problems.

Americans are more meticulous about their personal hygiene than the Arabs. Here, toilet paper is a strange commodity. Their sewage system is not designed to dispose of it. Consequently, troops before us had clogged up the plumbing. Tissue, if you were lucky enough to have any, had to be disposed of separately. Tissue purse-packs became a hot commodity among the women. Raw sewage was backed up everywhere we went. There was always water to stand in, sewage water and the ungodly stench that goes with it. It was particularly disgusting in the garages where meals were served. It makes me gag just to think of it even now, years later.

There were all kinds of personnel units in Kobar. Between twenty-seven thousand to thirty-thousand people filled one area. Feeding them was an enormous task. When we first arrived we were fed MRE's (Meals Ready to Eat) by the air force. We didn't know how good we had it until the Saudis or who we thought were Saudis, took over. Suddenly, mealtime became a real guessing game. *What is this?* you wondered. *Dare I put this in my mouth?*

One meal, breakfast, always included slime eggs and sausages that I refused to eat. The sausages looked like, well, I called them, "circumcised camel wieners." They looked uncooked, pale and white. I could not and would not put them in my mouth. Thank goodness an apricot or a bran biscuit was also available, or some of us would have starved. Mango juice was the juice of the war. It showed up at every meal. It was pulpy with very little taste. The coffee was outrageously awful. We drank it anyway, grounds and all.

Food was served buffet style. You waited in one line to get one item, another line to get the next item, and so on and so on. Hurry up and wait was the name of the game. While waiting, you talked to your neighbors, very small talk to make the time pass. "Hello! My name is Lieutenant Kwiatkowski, what's yours? What unit are you with? What do you do? Where are you from?"

One time while we were waiting in line, one of the servers, in the middle of dishing up a meal, threw up. Just like that! Oh, man...he threw up and kept right on working. It was awful. Surprisingly, no one got out of line. It's amazing what you'll put up with when you're starving. American health inspectors would have had a field day with the sanitation violations in this first encampment. It's amazing we didn't all die of dysentery.

We assumed we were being fed by the Saudis, but it was hard to tell. The nationals or locals as they were called—people from Pakistan, Sri Lanka, and other third world countries, actually cooked and served the food. In fact, they did all of the work, as far as we could tell. They were everywhere in their blue uniforms, carrying their little metal buckets. We never knew for sure what they carried in them. We assumed it was *their* lunch.

All the apartment buildings in the complex were surrounded with concertina wire and had armed militia stationed on the roof, barricaded in with sandbags and machine guns...protection against possible terrorist attack. One day several of us went up onto the roof to get a look at where we were. The Americans on duty, although kind about it, told us that it was not a good idea for us to be up there. We dutifully retreated, but not without taking in the view.

The panorama from the rooftop was spectacular. On three sides, as far as we could see, was sand. On the fourth side was the bay...the beautiful bay, the Persian Gulf. The sight of it brought tears to my eyes. *My son, my boy is out there somewhere. Maybe that slit on the horizon is his ship!* How long had it been since I had spoken to him or heard from him? *September? Can that be?* I struggled with the memory. So many things had happened. Just knowing he was so close was comforting, yet terrifying. It made me think of home. I was overwhelmed with a sense of loss. *Jesus, Mary and Joseph, protect him and his ship,* I prayed.

The days in Kobar were filled with drill, drill, drill. My unit consisted of nine women, nurses with varying degrees of training and experience. It was my duty to find out what each one knew and bring everyone to a certain level of competence and understanding. In the worst of times, I would have to delegate authority, and it was critical that I knew who could handle what.

My buddy, Grady, was an experienced RN (registered nurse) as was one other whose specialty was OBGYN (obstetrics and gynecology). Several other LPN's (licensed practical nurses) had vast knowledge. The LPN's, or 91 Charlies as they are affectionately called, are the work horses of the medical units. They are the ones who carry out the orders delivered by the RNs and the Ward Masters.

"We have to prepare for the worst! That's our mission, and we're going to carry it out to the best of our ability," I began. "Before we can do that, however, I need to know what the best of your ability is. I need to know exactly what I can expect out of you, and you need to know exactly what I expect out of you!" The words tumbled out of my mouth, as if I had been a veteran of several wars. "We're going to begin with a quick review of anatomy and physiology. Don't ask me any questions now. I expect you to already know these things." Thus began my first day of instruction.

That first day, the nurses in my charge looked at me with that cynical stare that screamed, "who the hell do you think you are!" I knew it would take awhile to gain their respect.

It was not my job to be popular. I had to make sure that my team was ready for anything, and I intended to do exactly that. The lesson continued.

"Land mine injuries involving the lower extremities and possibly the chest wall, might be common. If the chest wall is involved, the patient is not going to have much of a chance because by the time he or she gets to us, he or she probably will have bled to death." I covered possible injuries to the head, chest and extremities from bullets and knives, and phosphorus burns from grenades.

Next came a review of the arterial structure, the inner structure and the bone structure...what bones we might be looking at. Arrhythmia, pulses, what, when, and how. We talked about equipment available to us, and the equipment that we take for granted that we wouldn't have. For example, Doppler's, the machine that helps us listen to pulses, would not be available. Our fingers would have to be used to palpitate, instead.

We role-played every possible injury imaginable, from arrival of the patient, through standard procedures, possible complications and evacuation out, taking turns as patients. Role-play turned out to be the most effective of all the teaching tools we used.

We repeatedly enacted the consequences of modern day war. My responsibility was to make sure our unit knew what could happen to the body and how to react. The *why* wasn't important. "If you don't do what I tell you, then somebody's going to die, and if it's an American, then I am really going to be pissed! No American or Allied soldier is going to die under my care because of ignorance on our part!" I emphatically declared. So we trained day in and day out.

⊙   ⊙   ⊙

My faith was returning, slowly, out of desperation and fear. I searched daily for a purpose to my being sent here. I had to believe there was one. So, it was with great excitement that I readied myself to attend a service I had learned about.

The knowledge that a Mass was to be held, came my way strangely. Hosslern had gone with me to a podiatry clinic to see if anything could be done about the tendonitis I'd been experiencing in my feet. While I was in with the doctor, Hosslern went exploring. That's where she found it—a notice about a Mass being said the next evening in an apartment building near ours.

"Dare we go?" she asked thrusting the notice in my face. She saw my eyes light up as I read.

"Of course. Why wouldn't we?" I answered, excitedly.

"The rules...no females in male apartments! If we're caught, you know what the Saudis will do!"

"Screw the Saudis," I replied none too reverently. "This is church! Our church! Our God! We're going!"

The next evening, we approached the apartment building nonchalantly, as if strolling by. When we reached the door, we turned abruptly and ran inside. The elevator was guarded by a soldier holding an M-16. Startled by our entrance, he pointed it our way.

"We're looking for the church service," we said trying not to appear frightened.

"Okay. Fourth floor," he said, hitting the up button with the rifle butt.

Inside the elevator, we exchanged glances of confidence.

"So far, so good," I said. Hosslern nodded as the door opened onto the corridor.

The atmosphere inside room 427 was quiet, reverent, like church. We slipped into chairs joining seven others, all men. Introducing ourselves, we exchanged basic information only, name, rank, unit, etc. Most of the men were from infantry. No one said much.

Mass began shortly thereafter. The priest spoke of God's love and guidance through difficult situations, assuring us of God's greater purpose in sending us here. He challenged us to "keep the faith" as we struggled with our new surroundings. He was excellent. Father was from a parish in Long Island with 7,000 members. He shared his struggles adapting to the military, administering to thousands of troops, five people here, five people there....

Hosslern and I had taken a big risk coming to the service. It was dangerous for women to go out in the evening in Kobar. American women were being attacked. The Saudi decree that women were not allowed in male apartment buildings added to the danger. Regardless of the risks, I was so very glad we went.

Following the service, the priest offered to hear confessions. We stayed, of course. It was the first time since being deployed that I felt joy...true joy! I held onto that feeling for days. I didn't know if I'd be around for another service. As it turned out, we were not.

○   ○   ○

January 14th, we were given our first anthrax shot. We had no choice (even though many of us had concerns about what anthrax might do to our bodies). Anthrax is an animal disease characterized by internal hemorrhaging. The vaccine was *believed* to offer protection from biological warfare. But would it? Would the preventative be worse than the actual exposure? Some side effects were expected, but no one knew what for sure. The very issuance of the order frightened us all. Declaration of war was very close. We could feel it in the air.

Around nine o'clock in the evening, on January 16th, an eerie silence fell around the compound. The air was electric with anticipation. Those with radios were tuned to the BBC. President Bush and Secretary of Defense Cheney were making decisions. Cheney and General Schwarzkopf had gotten to-gether earlier. One of our young recruits voiced what we were all thinking. "Oh my God! What is going on?"

Then word came down to start taking the pyrastignone bromide pills. One tablet every six hours, on the dot. First the anthrax and now the pryostingmine. I tried to hide my trembling as I reinforced the orders. "Why?" was the question in everyone's eyes, but no one needed to ask. We all knew that these pills would minimize the side effects of chemical warfare. War was coming.

Pryostingmine in combination with anthrax has known side effects, but again no one knew for sure what to expect. One problem many had was increased motility, which basically means your bowels loosen and you end up with the "runs," horribly uncomfortable in the best of situations; traumatic in the midst of war, with your body encased in charcoal for protection.

An hour later the alert was sounded..."MOPP IV...MOPP IV... MOPP IV"! *Get into your chemical suits! This is it! This is for real! No more pretend. No more playing around. Jesus, Mary and Joseph, protect us all!"*

My heart beat wildly as I suited up. *Control! Control! Keep calm! Keep logical! You're responsible for the others. Don't panic! You'll be okay! Jesus, Mary and Joseph! Bless me O Lord for I have sinned. Help me get through this!* My mind raced trying to maintain a sense of logic, trying to suppress my emotions. *This is all a dream. The grandkids are coming over today and I'm taking them to the park. Now wake up. All is well.* Home was a distant memory, no longer real. *Don't sweat! Don't sweat! You need a seal on your gas mask! No seal, you die! Take your time. You've done this a hundred times. You can do this. Oh, Jesus, please, not yet! Don't take me yet!* Perspiration poured from my body as I suited up.

With gas mask on and sealed, I looked out at the blurry scene. *Corrective lenses! They promised them back in OBT, and they hadn't arrived. Damn! How am I suppose to see? How am I suppose to fight a war if I can't even see?* I cursed the army for its incompetence.

My God, here we are in this high-rise building sticking out like a sore thumb! Don't panic! No...no wait. The marines are poised ready to take Kuwait. It will be okay! I was talking to myself again. *Becky's friends, Wyatt and Shane, are in the First Marines. They've been here, somewhere in the desert since August. Jesus, Mary and Joseph, protect them.*

I thought about Wyatt, Mr. Tough Guy in his tattoos and leather, and Shane, so sensitive and gentle. I couldn't imagine him killing anyone.

The First Marines are ready to move. Please God, take care of them. And Dave, where is he? Will he be fighting too? My mind bounced from one thought to another. *The air force and the navy are starting bombing raids. It will be okay. It will be okay. Breathe! Breathe slowly! Calm down, look around. You are responsible. Others are counting on you. You can do this!*

Cocooned in MOPP IV readiness, I slump to the floor, surveying the others to make sure they were okay. *Well...make sure they're suited-up at least. It's impossible to tell if someone is okay in this get-up. I can't even tell what sex someone is let alone his or her emotional state.* I looked for overt signs of trouble.

Darkness, fearful darkness permeated the room. No one spoke out. Those with radios had them on, and I thought, *Oh my God, do I really want to listen to this crap?* Waves of terror wash over me, again. The stress of the moment was immense; rapidly rising and receding as I talked to myself. Up and down. Up and down my emotions fly. *Get a grip!* I started to pray, "Hail Mary and the Litany."

"United Air Force units have begun their bombing raids!" shouts the voice of the BBC with great excitement, "the war has begun!"

"Jesus, Mary and Joseph!" I exclaimed. "Okay guys, if you're going to do it, do it right! Blast the crap out of 'em!"

From outside, I could hear the sound of engines roaring as the military began it's move. *Get up, do something!* I

commanded myself. *You're in charge. See to your people.*
Struggling to stand, I forced myself to focus on each individual, attempting to determine his or her state of mind. I was especially concerned about the younger ones, those still in their teens. Through garbled talk and gestures, I determined that everyone was as well as could be expected under the circumstances.

When I got to Hughes, I couldn't believe my eyes. She was all suited up, calmly recharging batteries to her radio. "Hughes! What in the name of heaven is wrong with you?" I shouted through my mask. "We're in the middle of a war and you sit there recharging your batteries?"

"This is nothing, just wait!" she replied, laughing.

"This may be nothing to you, but man, this is real heavy for the rest of us," I shouted back. She shrugged and turned back to her batteries.

Hughes was a Vietnamese boat person as a child, so she was hardened to moments of terror. From her perspective, this *was* nothing. The parallel between what was happening to us at the time and what she was doing was ironic. I both admired and hated her for her ability to remain calm. In her narcissistic way, she was just taking care of herself. She simply blew off my reaction, and I was glad because I'm not a hateful person. I could feel myself becoming very goofy.

For several hours we went in and out of MOPP IV alerts. Into our chemical masks and out again. Most of us just left our charcoal suits on. It was easier. Sleep was impossible. We received no official word from the army that the war had started. What we knew, we had heard on the radio. We were aware of a cut-off point with the UN, but nothing else.

The start of the war would signal movement for the medical corps. Doctors and nurses would be sent off first to the hospitals that had already been setup, of that we were certain. With troops on the move, it was imperative that all medical staff be in place and ready for emergencies.

Orders came at 0300 to gather up our packs and report to the motor pool. We filed down together not knowing if we would remain as a group. We could be taken up north and dispersed to different units according to skills. We weren't certain what was about to happen.

When we were all assembled, the commander mounted a platform and gave us the news. "You're all going on a long convoy deep into the desert. Destination, King Kalhid Military City, affectionately referred to as KKMC. Each unit has been divided into three parties. The advance party is already there preparing for your arrival. Some of you will be left behind in the trail party. The rest of you will leave immediately. It is going to be tough, but I know you're all well-trained and that you will do your country proud. God be with you."

"KKMC, what is that? Where is that?" questions murmured through the crowd. "Deep into the desert. What does that mean? How far? How close will we be to the actual fighting?" No one knew.

When our unit was divided, Grady was put in the trail party. Allargo was with me. We were assigned to ride in an ambulance; somewhat more comfortable than the trucks. I was really frightened as we made our way through the motor pool area towards where the ambulance awaited. We walked gingerly, side-stepping holes and broken concrete, all the while watching out for the tanks, 5-ton trucks and Humvees that were getting ready to move.

"Which way, Allargo? Can you see the ambulances yet?" I asked breathlessly. My heart, beating rapidly, felt as if it would burst through my chest...a combination of physical stress from the 70 pound pack on my back, the emotional stress of being moved to who knows where and just plain gut wrenching fear.

"No...you okay still?"

"Yeah. Keep moving. I'm right behind you."

"It's over in this direction. They're lined up on the other side of the Humvees and 5-tons. I saw them this morning," she said moving forward.

Together we wound our way through the parked war machines to our assigned vehicle. All around us our comrades were doing the same. Few words were spoken. They were all lost in their own thoughts...their own secret terrors. The night was so dark, so quiet. Eerie.

KAABOOOM! A loud crash shattered the silence. Overhead flashed a bright light followed by flickers of colors. "Who's shooting off fireworks here?" I shouted. Sally looked at me aghast, her eyes wide with fright.

"Missiles! My God, Lieutenant Kwiatkowski, it's a missile!" A Patriot had intercepted an incoming Scud right over our heads! We stood stunned, unable to move, unable to think.

"MOPP IV! MOPP IV! Take cover!" came the mechanical voice over the loud speaker followed by the shrill, piercing siren. Everyone scattered, running for cover.

Allargo was already moving, gas mask in hand ready to put on. "This way, Kwiatkowski," she shouted, pointing. "There's a building over there, beyond the tanks." I struggled with my gas mask trying to follow her gaze. My heart was beating faster and faster. Breathing came in spurts. I began to feel woozy. My gas mask was on, but the lens wouldn't clear.

No seal! I can't get a seal! Oh God, No! Still struggling with my mask, I could feel my throat constrict. Gasping for breath, I begin to hyperventilate. *Calm down, calm down! Think! You can do this! Breath!* I commanded. Miraculously, my body obeyed. My breathing slowed. Re-adjusting the mask, the lenses cleared, but I was still nearly blind. The combination of the dark sky and the lack of corrective lenses rendered me virtually helpless.

"Allargo! I can't see!"

"Hold onto my belt!" she shouted, grabbing my arm. "Follow me." She guided me along, slowly, verbally, "one step up...now to the right...watch out for that hole." Together we shuffled around Humvees and trucks and tanks, in the direction of the nearest building. Soldiers were in the vehicles we passed, but they couldn't hear us. Patriot missiles took off right over our heads. We were scared to death. We were all alone. Everyone else had made it to shelter. It was dark, so dark.

Suddenly, my ankle twisted sending me sprawling. Now, on all fours, half in a hole and half out, I struggled to stand. My legs, paralyzed with fear, would not work.

"Get up!" commanded Allargo.

"I can't! My legs won't move!"

"You can and you will, Lieutenant! I'm not leaving you here alone to die. Now, move it!"

Allargo yanked on my arm. Rising slowly, I willed my legs to support me. Finally, standing, we stumbled towards the building. I couldn't feel or see a thing.

Seemingly out of nowhere, a masked person appeared. I heard a muffled, "Do you need help?"

Shaking my head rapidly, I yelled. "Holy Mother of God, Yes!" A strong arm grabbed one elbow, Allargo grabbed the other and propelled me forward into the building. Inside the foyer, we all collapsed on the floor. *Jesus, Mary and Joseph! Jesus, Mary and Joseph! Jesus, Mary and Joseph!* I repeat over and over again, to myself, trying not to cry, willing my eyes to stay dry. Relief for having made it to the building, and fear zap my energy. I swallow to catch a breath, my heart pounding in my ears. Even though others share the room, I feel vulnerable, totally alone. My emotions bounce in twenty directions. I will myself to be calm. Good air in, bad air out. Slow. Slow. Deep breath. You can do *this. You're okay, Dianah.* Slowly, panic subsided, logic set in, and I regained my composure.

The hallway we were in was filled with others dressed like us, military clones. Some stood, some sat. All were frightened. Allargo motioned to me that she wanted to move. I nodded. Slowly she got up and walked farther into the building. I followed on her heels. Suddenly, an explosion of light went off inside the building. My heart almost stopped. It took a moment to register that it came from a camera. "Who's taking pictures here?" I screamed through my gas mask. Another masked person turned and sat down.

Only after reaching a state of numbness, could I look around and comprehend the scene around me. It was surreal. *Monsters...frog men monsters. That's what everyone looks like...giant frog-like space monsters. Male? Female? It's hard to guess; impossible to tell. Everyone looks the same in these get-ups.* Allargo followed me as I pushed open a door and entered a room where three others were sitting on the floor. Joining them, I wondered for the first time, where the rest of my unit was.

Finally, the all-clear siren sounded, and we removed our gas masks. As hot and as stuffy as the room was, without our gas masks the air felt cool. After several deep breaths, I reach over and touch Allargo's arm. "Thanks, Allargo. I owe you one."

"Don't even think about it, Lieutenant You'd have done the same for me," she replied.

I was about to argue when a shout came from across the room. "Kwiatkowski! Allargo!" It was Hall, the OR nurse from our unit. Awkwardly we pull ourselves up and waddle over to where she had been sitting. The three of us immediately embraced, thankful to find each other. We began talking at once.

Before we could gather our wits and attempt to move outside towards the motor pool, the eerie wail of the siren began again. "MOPP IV! MOPP IV! Take Cover!" screeched the mechanical D.J. This time the message was interrupted with further warnings. "We're in line for a direct hit! Be ready!"

Dhaharan and Kobar were prime targets because Dhaharan was a port city, and the Third Armored, the First Armored and most of the medical corps were in the area; close to 30,000 troops. A direct hit would have resulted in massive loss of life and injuries.

Terror the second time around is no less frightening. Panic rose in my throat once more. My whole being shook as I struggled back into my chemical mask. This time it sealed on the first try. Instinctively, as if in a hurricane or a tornado, everyone moved farther into the building. Allargo, Hall and I huddled together. Clasping gloved hands, we began to pray.

"Our Father, who art in Heaven. Hallowed be thy name," came the words. "Hail Mary, full of grace..." Allargo wasn't Catholic, but I taught her "Hail Mary" anyway, just in case she needed it. Holding hands we continued praying, sometimes out loud, sometimes silently. We prayed for our survival and the survival of the others.

My prayers were very intense, very spiritual. I could feel myself lapsing into a deep meditation. Calm came over me. I felt light, as if I was being transported into another dimension. I could see clearly, no longer looking through the blurry lenses of a gas mask. *You're losing it, Dianah. Wake up!* I shouted at myself. *Stop this! You're hallucinating! Open your eyes!* But my eyes were open, and in the distance I could see a crowd slowly moving towards me, led by a very familiar face. *Mother? Is that you, Mother?* I asked unbelieving. It was she. *I miss you so much, Mom. Is it time? Did you come for me? Should I follow you?* The figure didn't say a word. She just nodded, smiled and floated by. I called after her, *wait, don't go!* But, it was too late. She had disappeared. Scanning the crowd once more, I recognized my dear mother-in-law and then my grandparents, Aunt Marge and Uncle Ben, other aunts, uncles and even a couple of friends who had passed on. No one said a word. They just smiled, nodded and moved on.

I didn't know what to do. Were they beckoning me? Was I supposed to follow? I started to pray even harder. Every prayer I had ever learned came to mind. I went through a whole litany of prayer, "Sacred heart of Jesus, Queen Mary, Mother of God...pray for me. Praise ye Jesus, I give glory to you. Hallelujah Jesus, I give thanks for the day. Saint Michael the Archangel, defend me in battle. Be my protection. Bless me O Lord for I have sinned. Hail Mary, Queen of grace. Now I lay me down to sleep." Forty-seven years of stored up prayers began to surface.

The prayers strengthened me. I could feel my faith returning. I'd experienced a vision with a profound message, been on a journey, without leaving the room. In the depths of my soul, it changed me. For the first time in my life, I felt a power greater than me was directing my life. I had the sense that I was being watched over and that I would be able to handle anything that came my way. It wouldn't be easy, but I knew I would survive. The fear was still there, but it felt different, somehow. It's difficult to describe. Attention returned to the room I was in, huddled on the floor, encased in rubber.

My new found inner strength helped me focus on the others in the room. Directly across from me, I noticed a small, gas-masked individual shaking. Even through the mask, I could tell it was a woman. She was crying hysterically. I motioned to Hall, and Allargo that I was going to crawl over and try to help her calm down.

"It's okay! It's okay!" I repeated, arm around her shoulder, fighting tears of my own. She leaned into me, shaking harder for just a moment and then slowly calming down. She was young, like my Becky and Mary. I suppressed the thought of them in a similar situation. After awhile, Allargo and Hall took over. While they talked to her, I made my way down the hallway checking to see if everyone else was okay.

Thank you, Lord for giving me the strength to help. I realized as I prayed that I hadn't even gotten the young girl's name.

When people are put into terrible situations, they do rally. Strength comes from somewhere, somewhere deep within. I'm convinced that my strength came from a Higher Power. I was physically exhausted, terror stricken and emotionally a mess before the Lord gave me a vision. There was no way that I could have dug deep within myself to come up with the strength to help that gal on my own.

Sirens continued throughout the night. Scud alerts came and went. We worked hard on the buddy system checking up on each other, making sure that masks were sealed and that water was being taken in; dehydration was a major concern. Water had to be taken in at regular intervals. Drinking through a gas mask is a tricky affair. But, we mastered it. It helped keep us busy throughout the night. Heaven help you if you had to go to the bathroom.

All through the night, I fought off tears. I talked to myself continuously, *Don't cry. You can't cry.* Crying messes everything up. I had to concentrate on being strong. It took every ounce of energy I had.

Even though future events would be more dangerous, this incident will always be one of the most terrifying in my memory. MOPP IV readiness was new, we were outside shelter, I couldn't see, and our missile retaliation was directly overhead and surreally alien.

When the all-clear siren sounded, we were rapidly herded out of the buildings to our assigned vehicles. The Commander was anxious to get us dispersed. We left in MOPP II readiness: pants, jacket, over-boots, just in case.

Our route took us west by northwest, out of Dhaharan into the desert on a two lane highway reminiscent of the wooden roads they used to have before concrete was invented. We moved in a huge convoy of trucks, ambulances and Humvees, heading down the highway in one direction with equally congested traffic going the opposite way. In the sand to the left of the pavement, the Third Armored, in their M-1 Tanks, tanks as big as a house, were moving into the desert. On the right side hundreds of Bedouins, their families, camels and goats were ambling to who knows where.

Winter is the rainy season in the desert. Nights are very cold, near freezing. Daytime temperatures soar into the 80's. All the while the winds blow, and it rains and rains.

It was a horrible ride; two lanes, no speed limit, a foreign driver driving like a drunk and nose-to-butt traffic. There was no security, no communication, no protection, and we wondered if the drivers knew where we were going.

The ambulance in which Allargo and I rode carried seven others. Talk aboard was idle...a joke now and then, otherwise silence. Many slept, but I couldn't. I needed to see where I was going. It had been barely two weeks since we arrived in this God-forsaken place, yet it felt like a lifetime ago. I wondered, as I strained to see out the windows, if there really was ever such a place as Ohio. *Did I dream I have children and grandchildren? Who am I? Where am I? This terror and fear, will I ever be without it? Will I ever get used to it?*

Rest areas are unheard of in the desert. When it became obvious that a pit stop was necessary, the ambulance would just pull off to the side of the road. No facilities, no privacy. Just you, the rain, the wind, the sand and the highway traffic. The combination of the pryostingmine pills and the anthrax shots created loose bowels in almost everyone, which added to the trauma of performing routine bodily tasks.

It was difficult, but we tried to maintain some kind of human dignity. First we removed our MOPP IV suit, then our regular clothing. We helped each other by making a poncho screen and took turns holding it up while each of us dug a hole in the sand and relieved herself.

Pit stops were few and far between. If we had to urinate in between, we used our dual purpose water bottle; drink the water, cut it in half and pee into it. Everyone in the ambulance was accommodating. We had to be. It was just the beginning of many little humiliations and indignities we were to suffer in the next few weeks. We were lucky, now. The ambulance was covered. Humvees and some of the other vehicles were open-aired or partially covered with tarps.

The convoy drove on and on and on. *Where are we going? When will we get there? How close will we be to the front lines?* All of these questions rattled my brain. I'm sure others were thinking the same things. *Oh, to be able to get out and walk around and then lay my head down on a cot in a tent somewhere.* The city rose up out of the desert in an imposing way. First it was a distant glow on the horizon. Then shapes and lights appeared. After sixteen hours of nothing but sand, the sight of it was overwhelming; like being on the "Yellow Brick Road," then suddenly coming upon the city. Affectionately dubbed, the "Emerald City," it reminded me of a futuristic space station on another planet. Finally, after approximately 300 miles and sixteen hours on the road, in the middle of a cold and rainy night, we pulled into the outskirts of King Kahlid Military City (KKMC).

KKMC was reportedly located in a triangular section near the Iraqi, Kuwaiti, Saudi border, about 60 miles from Iraq and 60 miles from Kuwait. The exact location was never officially confirmed. It is not a city as we know it. Rather, it's a military city, designed to train people for war. Huge concrete buildings interconnect with courtyards and walkways. Marble is everywhere. The entire city is ringed with fencing and towers for protection. Buildings are used for military training, and outside areas used for artillery practice. The Theater Mortuary is there as well as a huge cement factory. Special forces from all over come and go.

The King Kahlid Military Hospital exists within the city compound, set-up to handle 400 patients, primarily from the Allied forces. The 251st Army Reserve Unit was fortunate to pull duty there. They lived in villas within the compound in air-conditioned comfort. Their wartime experience would be very different from mine.

After circling the city for several minutes, our convoy pulled up to the area we would call home. Stiff-legged and sore from sitting so long, we anxiously climbed out of the ambulance into the cold rainy night, and looked around.

"God damned, son of a bitch" I heard someone utter. Other proclamations of profanity drifted through the silence. I looked around trying to focus in the dark. All I could see were the outlines of three tents! Three medium sized tents!

"This can't be right," I said to Allargo. "They've dropped us off at the wrong place. There's no hospital here!"

"God. There's not even a place to sleep!" she remarked.

"Where are the hospital tents?"

"We're supposed to be able to handle 400 patients! Where is the hospital?"

"Where are the sleeping tents?"

"Where do we live?"

"What are we supposed to do?" Questions echoed through the darkness as one by one military vehicles pulled up and unloaded.

There was no mistake. The advance party had arrived and set up three tents. A city of canvas awaited the rest of us in boxes and crates still loaded on trucks. As the reality of what all this might mean set in, the screeching wail of the sirens began to blow.

MOPP IV! MOPP IV! Take cover!

CHAPTER FIVE

"Enlarge the place of your tent. Stretch your tent curtains wide. Do not hold back. Strengthen your chord. Strengthen your stakes."

Isaiah 54

Scrambling back into the ambulance, struggling with gear and gas mask, I thought for sure the end was near. Through the darkness we could hear bombers taking off. *We must be near an airport,* I thought. The waiting seemed endless. I tried to block out the sounds, focus on other things, happier times thousands of miles away. I prayed. But my mind kept returning to what I had seen outside...three tents where a hundred should be. Three tents where a hospital should be. *What does it mean? Where are we? How close is Iraq? Do we have protection? What?* I couldn't silence the questions. It was January 19th, night time, somewhere in the desert.

When the "all clear," was sounded, we gathered our duffel bags and were herded through the rain towards the tents. Of the three standing, one had been designated male, one female and one supply/medical. These would be home for the next couple of days until the billet (housing) tents and the hospital tents could be erected. We were crammed in, sleeping bag to sleeping bag.

"Sleep," we were told. "Tomorrow will be a busy day."

Doing what, I wondered, praying that it wouldn't mean the obvious. Lying down, I tried to concentrate on happy thoughts. It was impossible. My thoughts were filled with terror.

Sleep was difficult. Whap...Whap...Whap...went the canvas flaps as the wind howled through the billowing tent. Strange smells, body odors mixed with damp canvas and wet sand, and sounds, distant motors roaring, assailed the senses keeping them alert, awake. The temperature dipped below 32 degrees. Part way through the night another Scud alert was sounded.

"MOPP IV! MOPP IV! Take cover!"

Once again, in the dead of night, still in my charcoal suit from an earlier attack, I reached for my gas mask. It sealed on the first try. Even so, I began to feel dizzy. Something was wrong. Breaths came in gasps. My heart was racing. *Oh, God, no,* I thought. *I'm losing control.* I couldn't believe it.

My arms reached out desperately clutching for anything, anyone that might help. It was obvious from my body language that something was wrong. A similarly clad officer came hobbling over to me, gripped my arms. Through my panic I heard a muffled voice.

"Lieutenant Kwiatkowski, get a hold of yourself! Think! Good air in. Bad air out. Good air in. Bad air out. You can do this. You're okay. Concentrate, Kwiatkowski! For God's sake, concentrate!"

I tried to follow her voice. My eyes wide with terror wouldn't focus. Incoherent mutterings came from my mouth. Internally, they made sense; a whole litany of prayers uttered all at once. Suddenly, a dull pain, a punch across my mask-covered cheek, got my attention. My vision cleared.

"Look at me, damn it! Look at me!" came the voice. "Now concentrate! Good air in. Bad air...that's right.

Slower. Slower. You can do this. Concentrate! Nice. Easy. Slow."

Focusing on her voice, I began to repeat with her, "good air in, bad air out." Slowly, my breathing returned to normal. Anne Hall was wonderful to me that day. We really didn't know each other well at that point. But, after she spent 20 minutes trying to calm me down, we felt like we were old friends.

"Thanks, Hall. I owe you one," I said, apologetically when the all-clear sounded. "Sorry I'm such a wimp!"

"Don't even think of it," she said. "None of us is immune. Next time it'll be me, you'll see."

It was my first and I hoped my last panic attack. I was very disappointed with myself for losing control. I never lose control. These type of things never happen to me, or so I thought. I've always been a strong, analytical person. Now I wasn't so sure. I'd only been in the desert for two weeks, and already I'd fallen apart twice. This time it was physical. I hyperventilated. A bonafide, classic panic attack. I was embarrassed and upset for having lost control in front of my fellow officers. *How will I survive the rest of the war?* I wondered. *Holy Mother of God, give me strength.*

As the days wore on, "falling apart" was not an uncommon problem. Each day someone else experienced it. We pulled together to help one another; no questions asked, no blame, just total understanding. Total support.

One more Scud alert interrupted our sleep that night. I handled it fine, falling asleep immediately afterward in sheer exhaustion. After what seemed like a blink of an eye, I was awakened to a strange haunting sound.

"Wwwweeeeaaaaaiiiiillll! Wwwwweeeeeaaaaiiillll!"

"Wha's that?" I yelled, jolting upright out of a dead sleep. Everyone else had heard it too. People were stirring and grumbling.

"Prayers," grumbled Allargo.

"Prayers?"

"The Saudis. Remember? In Kobar? Five times a day?"

"Oh, yeah. But, in Kobar, it was distant. Not like this."

"That's because they didn't blast it over the PA."

The wailing continued in a sing-song fashion for a long while. It gave me an eerie, sick feeling inside. I had always thought that I was tolerant of other religions. Apparently, I wasn't. I never got used to the evil feeling that came over me, five times a day. We were assigned to an area in the desert outside of KKMC, the military center for the Saudi Arabian defense forces. This was their home, their religion and their God, Allah. We would just have to get used to it.

Shortly after the wailing stopped, we were ordered out of our sleeping bags. With the dawn came the not so surprising news that we, the doctors and nurses, not the army corps of engineers, would construct the hospital. The air war had begun, and the ground war could begin at any moment. Time was of the essence.

The advance party had the plans laid down for the hospital and surrounding tents. This precise plan detailed how and where the hospital and all the billeting tents would be placed. It was our first task to stake out the plan in preparation for erecting the entire city.

For the next ten days our primary purpose would be to get the hospital up and running, as well as setting up the billeting tents for the staff. Reservists, doctors and nurses, untrained for this construction task were now performing backbreaking manual labor.

The tents were huge. It took about forty people working in precise synchronization to put one up. Normally, the army corps of engineers would come in, level the ground, and map out the location. This had not been done. Our commander felt that there wasn't time to call them in. We were ordered to erect the tents ourselves.

Huge trucks pulled up carrying canvas, ropes, stakes and poles. The canvas, was heavy and extremely awkward to move. If it were set down in the wrong position, it would have to be picked up and manually moved, an almost impossible task.

There were a variety of jobs for each tent erection. People were needed to level and stake the site, unload supplies, position the canvas, unroll it, secure the stakes and ropes, move and place the inner poles, fill sand bags and trench the outer perimeter to prevent flooding. People were needed to repair the tents. Some of them appeared to be left over from the Korean conflict and World War II. Those that had sections rotted out had to be patched. I unloaded supplies, carried canvas, placed the floor, the ropes, and the stakes. I did just about everything, moving from one job to the next as the tent went up. Everyone did. You didn't think about it. The job had to get done

The first day was the most difficult; officers shouting, then changing their orders. We wanted to believe they knew what they were doing. It was obvious they didn't. Rain and wind, complicated the whole process.

The first tent was the hardest to erect. Eight nurses and doctors were positioned on each of three telephone-sized support poles, ready to crawl under the canvas to put them into position. Twenty or more others were positioned around the base, readying the ropes and stakes. I helped haul the canvas from the truck and drop it into position. Now, I stood waiting for the signal to begin staking. Allargo worked beside me. Hall was across the way. Already my back was aching. All through the hauling I reminded myself to lift with my legs. *Use your legs.* It made little difference. The weight of the canvas made our 70-pound packs seem feather-light.

The three pole teams were poised, ready to hoist the tent, when another MOPP IV alert was sounded. Everyone dropped what he or she was doing and ran for cover, in the nearest tent. With no buildings around, canvas would have to do. Once again we sat, terrified, waiting for the blast or the chemicals. Praying for an "all clear" signal. We still didn't know where we were; how close we were to Iraq, or what kind of protection we had from surrounding units. When the "all clear" sounded, we lunched in the tent on MRE's and went right back to the rain soaked field, picking up where we left off.

There was a great sense of excitement and accomplishment as each tent went up. Like raising a circus tent, it was a production. When everyone was in place, the OIC (officer-in-charge) would shout, "One! Two! Three!" slowly, the eight people assigned to each of the three telephoned-sized support poles, in position under the canvas, would begin to lift them up as the rest of us pulled on our roped section.

Slowly the giant tent would take shape. There would be a moment of silence while placement was checked. When the "okay, it's a match," was given, the pounding and wrapping could begin, securing the tent to the ground. It was a study in teamwork. With each tent, the process went smoother.

When the first tent was up and secured, we all cheered. Somehow, in the midst of three more Scud alerts, we erected three more tents, four in all, that day.

Rain complicated the whole process in ways other than inconvenience. Desert sand does not absorb water. When water evaporates it leaves a base much like concrete, which makes the task of pounding stakes to anchor the tent ropes into the ground nearly impossible. Many mallets and stakes were broken trying to penetrate the soil. Because of the problem with the sand, the decision was made to abandon the important task of digging trenches around each tent...a decision that created worse problems later on, as tents flooded. The wind wrecked its own kind of havoc. We could never be sure that the tents would stay up.

Placement of each hospital tent was critical. Each had to connect to the next to form an enormous complex of interconnecting units. Miles of canvas fit together to form hospital wards, labs, supply rooms, hallways and all the various departments. If placement was off, even a few inches, zippers wouldn't zip, snaps wouldn't snap and ties wouldn't tie. Like a giant canvas erector set, slowly, day-by-day, tent-by-tent, we built a hospital in the middle of the desert. Slowly, the billeting tents went up also.

Since arriving in Dhaharan a couple of weeks earlier, we had had no contact with the outside world. So, it was with great excitement that we boarded trucks for a trip to the phone tents, ten miles down the road within the compound of another U.S. military unit. The PX, military store, was also there. These two locations would become very popular and familiar over the next few weeks.

The process for getting to the phone tents to call home was complex. First you had to find a truck to take you to the compound. Once there, you had to wait your turn on long lines. All military personnel in the area had access to the same phone tents, so there were always long lines. Then, when it was finally your turn, you could only make a collect call. If a connection was made and the phone started to ring, you prayed that the person answering would accept the call. Once a connection was made, you had only 15 minutes to talk.

My first call home was disastrous. All the way to the phone tents, I carefully planned what I wanted to say. But, when Tom answered the phone, I fell apart. I let everything out, screaming and crying and even swearing about all I'd been through, and how frightened I was. I couldn't tell him where we were, but I did say we were close to the front, and that we'd been Scudded four times that day alone, and that B-52's and helicopters were taking off over my head all day long. I'm sure I scared him silly. My son Patrick got on the phone and tried to be calm me down. Later he would recall it as "the phone call from Hell!" I was clearly out of control.

I was not the only one consumed with guilt after calling home. Many felt worse afterward. It's strange that the very thing that should have made us feel better, made us feel worse.

Much of the time I was too busy to think about home. Crazy as it may sound, it was easier focusing on the day-to-day, life and death struggles. Contact with home tugged at your emotions and your heart-strings. When you're busy and frightened and exhausted, you don't have time to think about what you're missing back home. Making contact brings it all back.

Mealtime in the desert was an adventure in itself. The first day we ate MRE's. After that, until we could get our own mess tent up and operating, MRE's made up two meals. For the third, usually dinner, we were loaded into trucks and taken about ten miles down the road to a large hanger, near the phone tents. There, along with hundreds of other military personnel from all over the world, we were fed a hot meal.

Our greatest fear during mealtime was getting lost and left behind. The mess area was huge and very confusing. We had to sign in according to our unit and keep track of our group, while filtering through several different food lines that emptied out into a huge eating area that could sit five to six hundred at the same time. Just like in scouting, the buddy system was a must. If we lost track of our unit, and the truck we came in, we would be left, stranded. Allargo was my buddy for that first meal.

Waiting in long food lines gave us the opportunity to interact with troops from all over the world. We struggled to break through language barriers. Some folks didn't want to talk. That was okay. Others couldn't stop talking. The first hot meal in the hanger was fantastic. Real food on a plate. No bag to open. I sat there enjoying my meal, chit chatting with Allargo and the others who sat at our table, all the while fully aware of the hundreds of others moving in and out of the dining area.

"Bet I can tell you which ones are medical," she challenged.

I looked around searching for tell-tale signs. "I know," I said, nodding. "No weapons."

"Yep!" she smiled. "You got it."

None of us from the medical unit carried weapons. Many of the troops having dinner had rifles and hand grenades, in addition to their MOPP IV suits, strapped to their bodies. The whole scene seemed unreal. I blinked several times, just to convince myself that I was really there. Suddenly, the sound of gunshots pierced the air.

Rat-Tat-Tat-Tat-Tat! An M-16 began firing rapidly.

"Hit the deck!" yelled Allargo. Steaming trays of food were left cooling table top as all troops hit the floor. Those with weapons readied them.

"Where's it coming from?" I asked. Allargo shrugged her shoulders. She was already busy trying to get her gas mask free.

"You putting your mask on?" I asked. She shook her head "yes." I looked around. Others were doing the same. We all waited for more gun shots, half expecting the MOPP IV sirens to go off, but neither happened. After a few minutes, conversation began to pick up as everyone tried to decide what to do. Finally, cautiously, we got back up and tensely resumed eating. No one ever explained what happened. Speculation was that a soldier had left his safety off, bumped it, and his weapon went off. No one knew for sure.

Once again our stomachs were in knots, our senses alert, adrenaline flowing. A chair would fall, and everyone would jump. We were spooked by everything, even thunder. Weather or attack? Amazingly, the sounds were similar.

That same day, after lunch, while waiting outside to board the truck back to our compound, a squadron of helicopters flew overhead, returning from bombing raids. They were so close, so low, I felt as if I could reach up and touch one. It made me shudder to think of where they had been. I felt as if I was in a "Star Wars" movie scene. Any minute someone would yell "cut" and send us all home.

Building a medical complex out of tents was not without its casualties. All of us suffered multiple medical problems from blisters and calluses to pulled muscles and strained backs, some more serious than others. Of particular concern were the surgeons whose hands were to perform delicate surgery. One slip of a mallet or pole or piece of heavy equipment could destroy their ability to perform their skills here and ruin their entire career after the war.

Physically, up to this point, I had weathered the hard labor pretty well. Some minor back spasms that seemed temporary. By the end of each day, I ached all over, and my hands, now callused, would never qualify for a hand-modeling career, but otherwise, I was holding my own. There wasn't time to be sick or injured. You got up and worked through the pain, or at least tried to.

My back gave out on the 21st. A storm had blown in off the desert with extremely high winds. While everyone else tried desperately to hold the tents down, I lay on a cot in tears, fighting back spasms. Hughes, the only one left in the tent, ran to get the doctor. Dr. Valdez, an osteopath and a masotherapist, arrived within a few minutes.

"Okay, Lieutenant, turn over," he ordered.

"I can't!" I said, tearfully. "Every time I move my back goes crazy." Answering his call for help, three fellow officers arrived to help turn me over. Once turned, Dr. Valdez began manipulating my back muscles. Between his massage and the drugs he gave me, I fell into a deep sleep. For two hours, I was dead-to-the-world.

A strange creaking sound penetrated my sleep. My eyes snapped opened, wide awake, alert. I didn't dare move for fear my back would spasm again. I felt somewhat better, but I didn't want to press my luck. I looked around trying to determine where the "creeek" sound was coming from. It was the beam in the center of the tent, swaying. The wind was howling outside. It moved the canvas up and down, in and out. Up under the canvas it crept, billowing the material. Ropes and stakes strained with the force. The creaking beams, all three of them, were swaying. Turning my head, I saw Hughes and two others busy at the other end of the tent. They seemed not to notice. The beam started to fall.

"Watch out!" I screamed, jumping up and running for the opening; pumping adrenline momentarily blocking the pain. Hughes and the others ran out the other end and were desperately trying to hold the swaying but still standing beams in place. I hobbled into the next tent hysterical, uttered a few profanities and screamed, "Isn't there anyone in there who'll help us with our tent?"

"We're trying to hold down our own tent," they shouted through the storm.

By the time I got back to our tent, others were there putting it back together. Between the back spasms and the pain medication, I acted irrationally.

The next day, the winds had died down and my back, though sore, was better, well enough to allow me to go back to work.

On January 22nd, we raised six tents. Late afternoon, a visiting Colonel stopped by to see how complete the hospital was.

"You are the most forward EVAC hospital in the war," he said. "Your job here is critical to the war effort. Our wounded will be brought directly to you. That's why we need this hospital up and running as soon as possible." His comments, meant to reassure, made us more frightened. No wonder we were being Scudded all the time.

It was rough going emotionally for all of us. Each day several would flip out, momentarily acting out in some bizarre way. The fear, the terror, the constant stress, coupled with the physical labor brought utter exhaustion.

The sense of evil that I felt when my foot first touched sand in Dhaharan was ever-present. The Islamic prayers blasted over the public address system five times daily offended my spirituality, and my Christian belief system. Normally tolerant, I lost all perspective the night of the 22nd.

For some reason, I was alone, outside the tent when the prayers began. With my water jug in hand, I started preaching, throwing water at this invisible voice that permeated the night air. "You know you're praising some kind of weirdo God named Allah, don't you?" I yelled at the top of my lungs. "A vengeful God! Not redemptive! Suffrage! Look around you. Your land, your people are being suppressed. You're not allowed to 'become.'" The prayers droned on. "Jesus Christ came for you to 'become!' That's what Christianity is all about! 'I am!' Your God says you are nothing!' Wake up, people of Islam, wake up!"

My ranting rousted several nurses from their tents. From somewhere a distant voice asked, "Kwiatkowski! What are you doing?" It was Hall.

"I'm casting out evil spirits! I can't stand these bastards!" I yelled again, continuing to throw water towards the speakers, trying to drown out the sound.

Hall backed off, watched from a distance.

"Let her alone," she warned the others. "She'll be okay. Let her work this out." Hall's Catholic heritage helped her understand what was behind my actions.

"Blessed be Jesus Christ and blessed be his Holy Name! Blessed be the true God! The true God! The true God!" I screamed. I got out my rosary and chanted along with the wailing. It was dueling prayers. Islam and Christianity side-by-side.

Finally, as suddenly as it began, the wailing stopped. The silence was deafening. It jolted me back to reality. I staggered, looking around. Stumbling, I made my way back into the tent, emotionally drained. Hall came up to me, gave me a hug and helped me to my sleeping bag. She said nothing. The others stared. I fell onto my bag, exhausted, and for the first time since arriving in the desert, I slept. The next morning, no one said a thing. Each day I was sustained by my faith. First thing in the morning and last thing at night, I prayed. All during the day, through the physical labor and especially during Scud alerts, and the prayers of Islam, I prayed. Each day I looked at the "Calendar of Saints" that Father Joe had given me, and laid my fears at the feet of the Saint-of-the-day. And, each day, in the evening before bed, I tried to write down a note or two about my experiences.

O   O   O

On January 23rd, in the middle of the night, the trail party arrived. A group of us got up to meet them. I was extremely concerned about Grady and Wagner, hoping that they hadn't been transferred to a different unit, or injured or even killed. They were so important to me...like family. Grady and I had made a pact that we would stick together in the event of an NBC attack; that we would always be there for each other. I had to make sure they were in the group.

The trail party arrived in a C-130 airplane. They had been packed in like sardines and were partially unloaded when the sirens went off.

"MOPP IV! MOPP IV! Take cover!" Sirens blared forcing us into the nearest tent. The arriving trail party, frantically turned and scrambled back onto the plane. What a welcome!

When I first saw Grady, she was extremely upset. She had fallen while walking off the airplane. In pain and carrying a 70-pound pack on her back, she was struggling to get up when the sirens went off. She panicked and couldn't make her legs work. A passing officer ordered her to get up or die, "right there on the spot." Somehow she had managed to get back onto the plane to wait for the all clear. When she finally reached the tent she was emotional. We hugged and cried and talked long into the night.

The trail party brought our numbers to almost 400, full staff for the hospital. The rest of the hospital complex went up rather quickly after that. As soon as a tent was up, crews began filling it with the necessary equipment and supplies;

cots, cabinets, chairs, desks, etc. We all worked 12-hour shifts to get the job done.

One by one the billeting went up, too. Once up, tents were assigned according to rank. Officers, captains and above were in one group, six to a tent. Then came the lieutenants who were housed 13 to a tent, and then the enlisted.

While the tents were being constructed, friendships were also building. Working 12 hours at hard physical labor gave you a real sense of the work ethics, moral values, temperaments, likes and dislikes of those around you. By the time tent #16 was readied, seven lieutenants, Hosslern, Grady, Wagner, Kocsis, Fisher, Allargo and I had agreed to share living quarters. We were joined by Jackson, Warren, Manos, Thomas, Smith, Holmok and Hughes.

And so it was that on January 25th, a day so rainy and cold that we could see our breath, thirteen women, all Lieutenants, all nurses, came to call tent #16 "home."

CHAPTER SIX

"Whatever God has brought about is to be born with courage."

Sophocles

The first six days in KKMC were so traumatic, I wondered how I would survive. I'd experienced sides of myself that I didn't know existed. They frightened me. The confident, self-assured, productive person that I thought was me seemed lost.

Moving into our tent, tent #16, "Sweet Sixteen" as we later named it, helped. For the first time since being deployed, I had a place to call home. A place to set down my things, and know that when I returned, they would still be there. Maslow called it the need for a semblance of order: a feeling of physical and psychological security. I hadn't felt a sense of security since deployment.

"Sweet Sixteen" was at the end of a row, near an intersection of tents, forty feet from two giant generators that ran 24-hours a day. It was so noisy we had to shout to be heard. We didn't care. We were happy to finally have a *home.*

Sweet Sixteen was a multicultural tent: one Vietnamese, four blacks and the rest white Anglo Saxon. Five gals worked with me in the Intensive Care Ward while the others worked in the Operating Room and the Immediate Care Wards. We were very fortunate that two, Kocsis and Fisher, were psychiatric nurses. It was like having our own resident psychiatrists. They were continuously intervening and listening when we had concerns or problems.

We moved our belongings in. The floor was dirt. We were thrilled. We were thankful to finally have personal space.

My bed space, 4' x 8' complete with a cot was to the right, the first one directly inside the tent flap. I had this thing about getting out in case of an emergency—windstorm or fire—plus I wanted to know who was coming and going in and out of the tent. No one argued when I grabbed it. Even so, I felt lucky to get it. The 200 watt light bulb that danced in the wind near the ceiling in the middle of the tent provided the only light. It cast shadows of rays on my cot.

Once my footlocker was dragged into place, I set about marking my turf. My sleeping bag was unrolled onto my cot. Pictures of Tom, the kids and grandkids, and the calendar from Father Joe were temporarily arranged on top of the footlocker until I could figure out something better. It wasn't until I brought out the moth balls that I'd packed, and carefully placed them in the corners of my space and around my cot, that I got a reaction from the others.

"Wheweee—what's that smell?" yelled Allargo.

"Is that you, Fisher?"

"Not me. It's coming from the door," she replied.

"Kwiatkowski, what have you gone and done now?"

"For your information," I replied sarcastically, "I'm protecting all of you from scorpions, cobras, desert rabbits and vipers. You can thank me for saving your hides from the desert varmints!"

"That may be, but does the whole tent have to smell like my grandmother's house?" asked Allargo.

"Ahhh—just trying to give our tent that "homey scent" I laughed.

That wasn't the end of the teasing about my moth balls, but I didn't care. We had to be so careful. The tent floor was dirt—sand actually—and home to hundreds of dangerous desert varmints. The moth balls must have worked because my end of the tent had very few desert visitors.

Each bed space started out quite sparse, but, day-by-day, as more supplies arrived, that changed. Thirteen women worked in diverse ways to "mark" their own territory. They all had the basics: cot, sleeping bag, footlocker, pictures of family and friends, a religious artifact or two and various cosmetics. We all had cosmetics of some kind sitting out as if to remind us of our femininity; nail polish, a tube of lipstick or two. They were seldom used. There was no need, no time to primp.

Trash picking became the favorite pastime. Discarded boxes and packing material provided juice for our creative minds. Sheets of wood became floors. Empty boxes became dressers, chests-of-drawers and desks.

My best find was white packing material that I rolled out onto the floor for carpeting, replacing the newspaper I'd been using to keep the dampness down. Everyone "oooohed" and "ahhhed" about it. In no time at all I also had a chest-of-drawers and a desk on which to place my toothbrush, toothpaste, medication, magnifying mirror, hairbrush, etc. I was even able to drape white linen material from the tent rope wrapping and tape up my photos of family and friends and the little things that people sent me. My bed space, like all the others, continued to evolve. Once we were settled into our tent, life seemed to normalize a little—as normal as serving in a war theatre can be with missile alerts interrupting your work at all hours of the day and night, and the ever present fear that any moment would be your last. We worked a few more days putting up the remainder of the tents, teaching the trail party who had just arrived, the ropes, so-to-speak. They got plenty of practice. Tents still had to be erected while at the same time many blew down in the windstorms that blew continuously over the desert sands.

Within a day or two of moving in, an announcement came that a shipment of mail had arrived. We all hurried over to stand in line for our first "mail call." My heart beat wildly as I waited, wondered and prayed that there would be something for me. There was: two letters, one from a friend at work and one from my niece, Susan. I cried and cried as I read the brief words. It was hard to see the words though the tears. I read them over and over and carried them in my pocket for days until the next ones arrived. It was so wonderful to know that my family and friends were thinking of me.

Mail call was usually followed by tremendous mood swings. It was devastating when you weren't among the lucky ones with a letter or package, and emotionally overwhelming when you were. Communication with loved ones back home was so important, yet contact ate through the protective wall we all erected to shield us from thoughts of home—the protective wall that kept us focused on the here and now and the work that needed to get done.

One of the more difficult things for fastidious, germ conscious nurses to adjust to was the facilities for maintaining the personal hygiene routines that we take for granted back home. I was in the desert for eight days before I got to take a shower, and that came about only because I insisted on being allowed to go. I'd been in my MOPP suit the whole time and was black from the charcoal lined garments, and I couldn't stand it anymore. (I don't remember having had a shower all the while we were in Kobar.) Our shower tent had not been installed as yet, so we had to be driven several miles to where massive showers were being shared by all the units.

The gal who accompanied me was someone ordered to do so. She didn't mind. She felt as I did—desperate for a shower. No one else from my unit was allowed to go. I felt fortunate.

The 5-ton truck bumped along the road in the black, black night. It was cold. We had no idea where we were being taken. Finally, somewhere near where we had been served food, we were dropped off and told to join a long line of women all dressed in full gear as we were—field jacket, Kevlar helmet, chemical mask, LBE, MOPP suit—holding a towel, clean underwear, soap and shampoo. Few had a change of clean clothes. It was enough to have clean underwear.

When our turn came, we were herded into an area approximately twenty feet square where we were directed to remove our clothes. Then, naked as j-birds, we joined another line—like pictures of women in concentration camps headed for the showers—that eventually walked into the showers. There was no privacy. You had to shave and clean yourself in front of everyone else.

It's difficult to describe how the hot water felt pouring over my body. I'd been dirty so long I'd forgotten how great being clean felt. I didn't want to get out. Who knew how long it would be until I'd be able to take another shower? I wanted to savor the moment. As it was, a few weeks later when our showers were installed, we would not have the luxury of hot water.

Showers were considered a luxury that could wait until all the billeting was in place. Latrines, on the other hand, had been in place when my troop arrived. They were located on the outskirts of the compound near the highway. They were open-aired and made you feel as if anyone passing by in a truck could see what your were doing. The latrines weren't totally open but felt as though they were.

It was dangerous going to the latrines, you never went alone, had to be ever mindful of the possibility of a Scud alert. The last thing you needed was to be caught in a compromising position when a MOPP IV alert sounded. The latrines did not provide adequate protection. Another reason for going with a friend was because the latrines locked from the outside.

Grady and I made it a point to visit the latrine after work and dinner, before going to bed. We would approach the makeshift facilities with our equipment in hand; toilet paper, handi-wipes and panti-liners. One evening, I was in need of some extra privacy and asked Grady to step back. Getting impatient, Grady agreed to step away promising to return. She walked away and forgot me. There I was locked in the latrine.

When I realized that I was locked inside, I began calling quietly, "Grady? Grady? Where are you Grady? This isn't funny!" I didn't want to yell, I could attract the attention of one of the nationals running around, and that wouldn't be good. It was pitch black outside, and I was getting pretty scared. If I'd have had a pistol, I wouldn't have felt so vulnerable. Finally, I saw a tall dark figure walking by. I knew by the size that it had to be one of us so I called out, "Excuse me! Excuse me! Could you please unlock the door?"

When I got back to the tent, I let Grady have it. I was really pissed. She just plum forgot that I was in the latrine. Later, the more we thought about it, it became funnier and funnier.

CHAPTER SEVEN

"For when your patience is finally in full bloom, then you will be ready for anything; strong in character, full and complete."

James 1, verse 4

"Please ma'am, can me and my buddy have a cigarette?"

The voice wavered, almost a whisper as he nodded towards the next cot. His blue eyes were big, drugged, intense, piercing. They were the eyes of a twenty-year-old, aged by war. He and his buddy had been brought in together; been together when the explosion occurred. Both had just had surgery; debriedement and restructuring of their hands. Young, in the prime of life, now facing years without hands. My heart lurched.

When the request came for a cigarette, both young soldiers were fresh post-ops. Although lucid—only gas was used during their surgeries—they were both in a great deal of pain and needed constant observation. The general practitioner (GP) on duty, at my request, had over-ridden the orthopedic surgeon's orders for pain killers. A strong form of codeine, headache medicine taken by mouth, in my opinion, did not seem appropriate for the pain of reconstructive surgery. The GP agreed with me. He had been in several wars and understood the pain and the psycho-social problems that accompany war injuries. The pain shots he had just administered were taking effect.

Oh what the heck, I thought. *After what they've been through, they deserved a smoke.*

Equipment in the ward, oxygen especially, made smoking prohibited, so Wagner and I wheeled them outside into the night air, on carts. They took long draws on the cigarettes we held to their lips. In between we sucked on our own. Few words were spoken. It was enough to get through the moment. What do you say to twenty-year-olds who have just lost their hands? How do you convince them that life without hands would be fine? How do you chit-chat? What could I say to these young men? Words of encouragement seemed so shallow. We smoked in silence, lost in our own thoughts.

Trails of smoke circled upwards from our silent foursome outside the I.C.U. tent; upwards towards bombers taking off and helicopters landing, upwards towards incoming Scud missiles and the Patriots that destroyed them, upwards towards the zillion stars that twinkled peacefully above in the night's sky. We stood, lost in thought, slowly nursing each puff.

We had been working 12 hour shifts in the hospital since the 3rd of February, still setting up tents, cots, meds, and role-playing injuries. Orders had been given to get the hospital up and functioning ASAP. The air war was escalating. Saddam had moved 60,000 troops to the border, four planes had been shot down, a U.S. female had been captured, and the U.S. had suffered the first casualties in ground fighting— marines had died in a friendly fire incident.

Maneuvering through the day with the weight and bulk of a helmet, gas mask and MOPP IV suit dangling from my belt was becoming familiar. Still, I struggled through the long hours of hard physical labor, longing for the routine of regular medical traumas.

I was as cooperative as my body would allow. It didn't last long. My back acted up again, so I was reassigned, from heavy tent building to laundry duties. I only lasted a day. My back couldn't take it. The laundry facilities were bad. Underwear came in white and went out brown. I knew right then and there that I would be hand washing my things.

The day the hospital opened, two tents blew down. It was amazing that more didn't. We were in the midst of the worst sandstorm we'd experienced since arriving. Stinging, shifting sand was everywhere, in every nook and cranny; annoyingly present in everything we did and every move we made.

Covered in canvas, my jacket over my head, I stumbled blindly in the direction of the hospital. Thank goodness Sweet Sixteen was so close, I thought. Everything fell into place like a well-oiled machine. Like hospitals everywhere, doctors called the shots and nurses followed orders.

Our mission in ICU was to stabilize patients enough to EVAC them to a backup hospital in Landstuhl, Germany, where, depending upon the extent of their injuries, they would be shipped home or on to another hospital in the country of their origin. The two young men, who had lost their hands, our first patients, would be Germany bound, soon.

Most of the 40 beds in our unit were occupied everyday. Unlike hospitals back home, patients weren't shifted from ward to ward as they got better. Here, they were packed up and shipped out.

Initially, we cared for very few battle related injuries. Although the air war was in progress, the ground war was still in the "talking" stage. All of our patients had serious illnesses or injuries related to preparation *for* war, from living in a military community and from the hardships of living in the desert. Before the war was over, we would see patients from the

United States, the Allies, enemy prisoners of war (EPOWs) and civilians. I was most surprised by the civilians. Men, women and children flocked to the hospital with a variety of physical ills. They came in vehicles, on foot and by camel from all over Saudi Arabia, Egypt and even Iraq.

Within the framework of the ICU, different areas were cordoned off. We tried to keep the Alpha area for the American injured. Allies were placed in a different area, civilians in still another, and, when the EPOWs (enemy prisoners of war) started to arrive, they were put in still another area. Even though our patients were in serious condition, side-by-side placement would have led to chaos.

"Lieutenant Kwiatkowski, you're needed in the Alpha area, stat!" came the call.

David, a 38-year-old black man, brought in with severe chest pains, had to be monitored closely while the head nurse went to lunch. Accessing what might be causing the chest pains was difficult, because it was so hot and so many people were dehydrated. Dehydration sometimes leads to chest pains. We didn't have the equipment to do the lab tests that would have identified specific coronary problems. Our only method of discerning the difference was to observe and monitor.

Without a word, I sat down, picked up David's huge dark-skinned hand, and began massaging first his fingers, then his arm. Huge, dark, frightened eyes watched my every move. He said nothing. His breathing was painful, shallow and tight. I sat in silence for a few minutes and prayed.

"I want you to relax. Just relax." I then said calmly. "Imagine you're floating somewhere special. Everything is calm. You feel totally at peace."

His fingers loosened their grip as tension oozed out of him. It was working. I wasn't sure it would.

"Now, David, think about the vessels in your heart." He tensed for just a moment, and then relaxed again. "Imagine the vessels opening wide and the blood easily flowing through. You're feeling better and better and better." Slowly the tension lessened.

We talked for awhile after he calmed down. He was the aide to a general. He was embarrassed about his chest pains and in complete denial that they could be anything serious. I assured him that his boss had done the right thing by bringing him in; assured him that we would get to the cause.

"I was praying for you when I first took your hand," I said. "I prayed that the Lord would alleviate your anxiety. To heal, you need to be calm. I believe that the Lord sent you here for a reason, and that he is going to take care of you." He nodded his gratitude.

The general, David's boss, was very concerned about him and very attentive. Whenever he came in, David tensed up, partially because of rank and respect, but mostly because he didn't want to appear weak in the general's eyes. The energy he wasted trying to reassure his boss wasn't good for him. I understood the reasoning, but I couldn't allow it to continue. David had to remain as calm and relaxed as possible.

"Sir, would you mind leaving him alone?" I asked the general politely. The general looked startled at my request. "With all due respect, sir, whenever you come in, he immediately tenses up. We must keep him as calm as possible until we find out the root of his pain."

"I understand, Lieutenant. Whatever you think best. You're in charge here." With that he saluted and walked out. The LPN on duty in Alpha area came running over. "I heard what you said, Kwiatkowski!" she exclaimed. "My God you've got guts. You told a general to leave!" She seemed incredulous.

"This wasn't about the general," I replied annoyed at her reaction. "It was about our patient. I saw what the general's visits were doing to him. A patient's well-being must always come first!" I declared.

If the truth be known, I surprised myself by speaking to the general the way I had. I could see that his concern was genuine but that he had no idea that his visits were upsetting his aide. Once I pointed that out, he was as gracious as he could be.

It was difficult to discern the difference between anxiety, fear and actual pathology. Everyone was pushed to the max; gender was not an issue. Everyone pretended life was okay, job was okay, emotion was okay. I think David was having that problem. He was trying to be everything to everybody on top of being the general's attaché.

Doctors floated in and our of our units on a regular basis. We were never quite sure where they came from or where they went to when they left; if they were reassigned to another unit or shipped home. Our unit worked closely with surgeons, and we had many, many good ones. They came in all different sizes, shapes and ages. The oldest I remember was 72 years old. Dr. Taylor, a general practitioner (GP). I didn't have much contact with him, since he was in the wards dealing with illnesses such as asthma. (Asthma was a major problem in the desert because of spore-forming organisms. They lay dormant in the sand until the sun hit them, forcing them into the air where they attacked lung tissue.) Doc Taylor was memorable because he fell off a 5-ton truck and broke a couple of ribs. *Would he be sent home?* we foolishly wondered. Of course not, his colleagues wrapped him up and sent him back to work.

Most of the doctors were like Dr. Steen, in their 60's, Vietnam veterans and orthopedic surgeons. Our resident "suit" however, was a GP. Trained as an osteopathic doctor, his ability to manipulate bones was invaluable. I speak as a colleague and a patient.

One of our surgeons was of Arab decent and was having a terrible time coming to grips with fighting Iraq in Arab territory. He became suicidal after the death of a young Arab found in the desert and brought in for care with the first group of mass casualties. The patient, Abdul, was a handsome, 26-year-old, who was the image of artists' portrayals of Jesus: his long dark hair and piercing eyes. All he needed was a crown of thorns to complete the picture. How unsettling and how ironic it was that this Muslim soldier carried the face of our most beloved Christian Deity. Abdul had been shot, and was dying from DIC (disseminating intra-vascular coagulation) which meant that he was bleeding to death internally. I beseeched the doctor to try Heparin therapy, a relatively new approach that research recommended as a last ditch effort.

"No!" he said adamantly.

"But he's going to die anyway. Why not try it?" I protested.

"He's not going to die! Who's the doctor here?" he asked. The doctor had never heard of the treatment, and he didn't trust that a nurse, such as I, would have that kind of knowledge. So, I had to sit and watch this young man die.

"Am I going to die?" asked Abdul through an interpreter.

"Yes," I nodded sadly. "The infection. Soon. If we can't get it under control."

The interpreter did his best to make sure Abdul understood. He accepted my honestly with dignity. He seemed to relax.

"If we can't control your infection, is there someplace or somebody I can have your body sent to?" After the interpreters asked my question, there was a long pause.

"To my wife, in Baghdad," he said haltingly, and made hand gestures like he needed a paper and pen. Then, with great difficulty, he scratched an address. Before Abdul died, I told him that I was going to pray my Christian prayers for him. Perhaps he was too far gone to object, but he didn't seem to mind. He had been a teacher: a learned man, highly educated and intelligent. I prayed that he would drop into a coma and go peacefully. But sadly, it was not to be. We kept pumping the blood into his veins, and he ended up drowning in it two days later.

When Abdul's doctor finally realized that Abdul was dying, he became suicidal and disappeared from our area.

The hospital, once up and functioning, was visited by officers and commanders alike; all asked questions.

"Do you think you're capable of handling mass casualties?" Inherent in the question was the frightening message: the potential was there and expected soon.

"Yes, without a doubt," I'd confidently reply. "Of course, if you have 40 mass casualties coming in at once to any unit, you're in trouble wherever you are!" I'd always add. Little did I know that my confidence in our ability would be tested within a few days.

○   ○   ○

My name showed up on the roster for the first go round of night shift duties. I was coming off three days in the hospital ER with a very bad case of food poisoning. Doctors stateside would have ordered me home to several days of bed rest. Here a nurse had to be almost dead to get bed rest.

That night I listened as tiny sand pellets pelted the canvas that sheltered us. It stung its way into every nook and cranny of our being, making it hard even to breathe. We ate it, slept with it, washed in it. It was in our hair, our ears, behind our knees and under our nails, gritty, black and ugly. Physically weak and totally exhausted, I reluctantly left Sweet Sixteen, in the middle of the worst sand storm we'd experienced. And Saddam's military had bombed fifty Kuwaiti oil wells sending black soot and oil into the air to intermingle with the sand, leaving a black, sticky soot on everything. I hunched over in an attempt to keep the blowing black sand from invading my body as I made my way towards ICU, all the while thinking about how I used to grouse about sand between my toes after a day at the beach. *I'd never complain about our dry, warm, light sand again, once I got home,* I promised myself.

The air war was in progress for almost a month, and the ground war had just begun. Saddam Hussein responded positively to a Soviet peace initiative in an attempt to avoid a ground war, but the United States had held back. President

Bush gave Saddam until noon, Saturday, to get out of Kuwait. When he did not, early Sunday morning, February 24th, the allies launched a full-blown ground attack.

I'd been working the shift for several days when we got the call from Bosra, from the MASH unit, that mass casualties were on the way. Captain Zellers put out the call for twenty more personnel, three or four plus Captain Middleworth, our other head nurse, in our area alone. We attended to the patients already under our care and awaited the deluge.

We wondered who the wounded would be. "Please, God, few Americans. Don't let them *all* be Americans," I selfishly prayed.

The mass casualties were transported to us in buses and helicopters in the middle of the night. We could hear them coming. Even amidst the loud hum of the generators that provided electricity, the roar of jets taking off and landing, and the many other loud noises we'd become accustomed to, we could discern the different sound. The constant drone of the motors of a parade of buses pulling in was unmistakable; the white, seatless buses, filled with litters carrying severely injured people.

The ER got them first then triaged the most serious to our space. Fifteen arrived in the first wave. Most were EPOWs (enemy prisoners of war), and they came with armed military police (MP).

Working on the EPOWs, even when they were on ventilators, unconscious or severely injured, was dangerous and difficult. We had been given no training related to their beliefs and practices. We were not told that they had been brainwashed to believe the evil Americans would use them for medical experiments, torture them and even drink their blood.

Nor did we realize the extent to which their religion taught that American women were evil and of the Devil...that to be touched by an American woman was to be touched by the Devil himself.

Tent sides were hastily rolled up as the litters were dragged in amid the instant chaos of orders being shouted, men moaning and screaming in pain. The stench was almost unbearable. I saw Jacobs cover her mouth and gag. McGrath turned almost as green as the tarnished leprechaun dangling from her neck when she saw our patients were EPOWS.

"We weren't supposed to have Iraqis!" she protested.

"Well we got 'em," I shouted, "now get to work!"

Later, I learned that rumors had circulated amongst the LPNs and lower ranks that we wouldn't have to deal with the Iraqi prisoners. Where that false rumor started, no one seemed to know.

The first order of business was to strip each EPOW, check for guns, knives and any projectile that could be used as a weapon. Next we would clean them up, remove old dressings and such, and ready them for the doctors moving swiftly from cot-to-cot shouting orders. In addition to their injuries, mostly gun shot and explosive related, their wounds, sand infested and crusted over, oozed with infection and infestations of lice. There were many back injuries. Saddam's Republican Guard, in an attempt to force his soldiers forward into battle, shot his own soldiers. Many were among this first batch of prisoners.

EPOWs who were lucid, fought our every move. Move slightly in their direction and they would start ranting and raving, swinging any appendage possible to keep us away. MPs with M-16's poised for action, moved with us from bed to bed so we could perform our duties. It was absurd. It tested my dedicated, caring, sensitive, caregiver nature. Here I was living in hell, working my butt off for men who didn't want me to touch them. It was difficult to hold back the, "who gives a damn," attitude. I prayed my way through that day as I did most days and nights.

As unsettling as is was to work with MPs all around, we knew and appreciated them every second that they were there. There's no doubt that without them, many of us would have been hurt, raped or worse. The unadulterated hatred in the enemies' eyes that followed us through our daily tasks left no doubt.

From that night on, mass casualties came in on a regular basis. With each new batch of EPOWs came all the fears, the battles, and the massive injuries. It became normal, comfortable, essential to have an MP at our elbow, as we made our rounds.

"Can I have some help over here?" I yelled at the MP sitting on a chair one bed space over. The Iraqi in the cot I was working on was carrying on something fierce. He'd been unusually belligerent throughout the night and had been tied down—hog-tied in straddled position. I was trying to give him a shot to calm him, when he began thrashing uncontrollably again.

The MP didn't move. I yelled again, "Hey...I need help!" Still, he didn't move.

"Damn...the MP is asleep!" I said out loud, furious. Quickly and quietly, I moved to the chair where he sat and gingerly took his M-16 out of his hands. Pointing it directly at his head, I nudged him. He woke up with a start. Eyes wide. Frightened. As damn well he should have been.

"I could shoot you, right here...now!" I said trying to control the anger in my voice, as I moved the gun to an upright position. The MP sat frozen, alert. He stared at me. "I don't expect you to fall asleep!" My voice rose as I continued. "I'm tired too. We're all tired! But..."

"What seems to be the problem, Lieutenant?" Captain Marks had come into the bed space without my knowing it. With eyes stilled glued to the MP, I said, "Get him out of here, Captain. Just get him out of here."

O   O   O

Patients remained in ICU only as long as necessary. Turnover was fast because we had to continually recycle them. One patient blended into another from one trauma to another. But a few patients were memorable.

Abdul, of course, and another young, 17-year-old resistance fighter particularly.

It was his hazel eyes that impressed me. I asked him about his family. Had they been from northern Iraq? Had they intermarried? He didn't seem to know.

The patients that really pulled at our heartstrings were the children. One beautiful young girl around 11-years old, had a bomb explode on her chest which blew her leg off. She'd picked the bomb up, even though she had been told not to touch anything that looked unfamiliar. Amazingly, she survived. We patched her up and shipped her off. To where I don't know. *What future is there for a young woman with only one leg in that desolate land?* I worried. It was hard to let go of her image.

That child, along with many other injured Iraqi civilians, were brought down from Bosra. Iraqi hospitals had all but been shut down, so they came to us. Even Saddam's brain-washing couldn't keep them away. They knew there was food here, three meals a day and shelter. When people are hungry, they'll chance most anything.

All the while we worked, the winds blew. Some days were worse than others. There was always the threat that at least one tent would blow down. All the while we worked, temperatures fluctuated from very cold, near freezing evenings, to sweltering hot days. Torrential downpours complicated life even more. Totally unlike the storms I was used to in Ohio, these rains turned sand to concrete, making each step difficult, slippery. They drenched clothing and dampened belongings in our tent houses. Rains that flooded floors made you thankful for a cot to sleep on. The memory of the smell of damp canvas and wet sands will forever be with me.

Burning oil wells a bit more than 60 miles away threw pungent odors and strange fumes into the air, fumes that stung eyes and made breathing difficult. Our lungs protested with a mild burning sensation each time we drew a breath. There was no time to contemplate the consequences of the air we were breathing. The sky eastward towards Kuwait was black with soot. Its oily, sticky base settled on everything.

All the while we worked, filled with ever-present fear. It wore us down. While we struggled with ventilator tubes, kept hearts going and treated bleeding and gaping human flesh, Iraqi Scuds exploded nearby, intercepted, thank God, by our Patriot missiles. Work stopped routinely, although only momentarily, while we jumped into MOPP IV gear. Encased in charcoal suits, thick rubber gloves and gas masks, we were becoming proficient at most nursing functions. Being busy during these alerts helped take our focus away from what might be in the warheads exploding nearby.

We did our best with our patients when Scud alerts sounded. Recommended procedure wasn't practical most of the time. It's difficult to put a chemical mask on and move patients down under their cots when they're hooked up to monitors and IV's. That procedure alone would have resulted in the deaths of many of them. Instead, we did the best we could.

The EPOWs did not like us in MOPP IV readiness. They were terrified. Where were their masks? How were they to survive? They had been brainwashed to believe that their leader had the ability to eliminate the Western powers. They knew of the weaponry he had.

CHAPTER EIGHT

"No fine work can be done without concentration and self-sacrifice and toil and doubt."

Max Beerbohm

There was no such thing as a typical day in the desert. Everything about living was atypical. But, with the hospital up and fully functioning, days settled into a somewhat regular routine.

Day shifters awoke at approximately 5:15 A.M. and night shifters around 5:00 P.M. Half the tent worked the same shift as I, the night shift.

Dueling alarms woke me late afternoon. Focusing groggy eyes on the canvas flapping overhead, my first thought most days was, *Thank you God for helping me to get some sleep and giving me another day.* Reaching over, I'd grab my rosary praying first to Saint Michael the Archangel to defend me in battle and then a prayer of thanks and a plea for protection and strength to handle whatever came my way that day. I'd end my daily prayers with, "Lord Bless and keep my family; Tom, David, Patrick, Mary, Rebecca, Jackie, Francis, Ann, Nick and little Tommy, and for all the people that I've forgotten about who asked me to pray for them."

With a quick glance at the floor to make sure we hadn't been flooded while I slept, I'd reach over, uncover my boots and give them a shake. Then, when no unwanted visitors re sponded to the flashlight beam shone down inside, I'd pull them on, lace them up, stand up and stretch. I never took for granted whose home we were living atop of: scorpions, deadly vipers and other kinds of pests. As cozy as we were able to

119

make Sweet Sixteen, we were the intruders in a thriving desert alive with creatures above and below the surface. My secret weapon was moth balls.

Shaking out boots followed by the wash down were important first steps to morning. Panty liners were used for cleanliness and sanitary purposes, after washing up with Handi-wipes™ and bottled water. There wasn't much else to getting dressed, because we seldom took our clothes off. Makeup was a waste of time in the heat, the wind, sand and rain. Outside of a few who applied nail polish, just to feel feminine, no one bothered. To complete the morning wakeup ritual, we'd go outside the tent with toothbrush, toothpaste and water bottle in hand, to brush our teeth. The trench dug around the outside of the tent to divert water during rainstorms, was our sink. Primitive? Yes, but it worked. It was all we had. We adapted.

My last act before leaving the tent was to roll my sleeping bag up tightly. After working 12 exhausting hours, I didn't want to crawl into my bed and find a visitor waiting for me. Then, with a kiss hastily blown towards the family pictures smiling from my cardboard dresser, I'd head out the flap, towards the MESS 5:45—6:00 p.m.

Once out, I was off to the MESS tent to stand in line for my breakfast, which was dinner for everyone else. I could never be sure what the fare would be. On rare occasions, breakfast food would have been saved for those of us who worked the night shift. Supplies were limited, so we never knew if we'd have real cooked food or MRE's. It varied from meal to meal, day to day. There were few complaints, however. We were grateful for food to eat.

Meals in the MESS provided food for the soul as well as the body. It gave everyone a chance to interact with other military persons stationed together. Human nature gravitates towards the familiar, and waiting in lines forced circles to widen. I was constantly fascinated by the variety of people that this war had brought together.

7:00 p.m. —7:30 a.m. Night Shift. My shift began by interacting with the outgoing day shift RN's. who handed over a report providing up-to-date information on new admissions and each patient's progress during the day. The RN couldn't leave until we had discussed each patient thoroughly.

Shifts in the hospital were never routine, each moment was peppered with the possibility and the fear of incoming missiles. Depending upon the patients, injuries, numbers of gas masks and protective gear available, following MOPP IV patient procedure became a judgement call. For me, there was never a question about putting on my full MOPP IV gear whenever a Scud alert sounded. During the days of air and ground attacks, the alerts came regularly, several times a day. Others got lazy as the war began winding down. I, however, wasn't about to take any chances with my life. I couldn't help anyone if I wasn't protected.

Once we started to get EPOW's, our stress levels rose rapidly. Everything became more complicated. Administering to patients who would just as soon kill or rape you was frightening. As one of two RN's in charge, I had to make sure that other nurses in my charge were well protected and supported. Iraqi EPOW's didn't know the meaning of the word "gratitude."

Lunch and dinner during shift was "catch-as-catch-can." There's an old army saying that fit each day. "Eat when you can and sleep when you can because you don't know when you'll get the chance again." Sometimes there was time to run over to the MESS tent, but most often I would pick up MRE's during breakfast or the previous meal, and bring them to work, just in case. We also brought to work food that had been sent to us by family and friends. Canned tuna fish and Cup-A-Soup were luxury meals. Even when we had a chance to run over to the MESS, the long wait in lines would eat up time so we'd have to run back to eat at the ward. The amount of time allocated for meals depended upon our number of patients and how far behind or ahead of schedule things were.

Mail Call was a problem for everyone, especially the night-shifters. Since hours for pickup were limited to daytime only, we'd have to set our alarms and interrupt what little sleep we got, to run over and see if anything had our name on it. Even when working the day shift, we'd have to wait for a lull in duties to take the time to run over. On my shift, we would always try to rotate duties so that each of us could make a "quick trip," even though we knew that there was no such thing as a "quick trip."

When the mail started coming in, late January, it was so good the hear from my family and friends. In addition to family stuff, they asked detailed questions about the war that surprised me. I had no idea that people back home knew so much about what was happening. They seemed to know much more than I or any of my colleagues. The only information we got came over the BBC—British Broadcasting—a wizard station 106. The idea that CNN was broadcasting around the clock never occurred to us.

When night shifts were over, RN's had the responsibility of transferring patient information to incoming day staff. Both the LPN's as well as the two RN's on duty had to finish up with their patients before they could leave. Consequently, even though shifts ended at 7:30 a.m. We seldom left the hospital ward until well after 8:00 a.m.

8:00 A.M. Free Time. Once my shift was officially over, I'd hurry back to Sweet Sixteen, grab soap, towel, shampoo and clean underwear (if I was lucky to have some), and make a mad dash to the showers before the female shower shift was over. Showers were shared by all, so the hours were closely regulated.

The showers were "gang" showers where modesty was a thing of the past; privacy non-existent. I'd wait in long lines with a huge group of females, mostly strangers. Occasionally, I'd see a familiar face, but usually we'd pass the line waiting time by introducing ourselves and exchanging bits and pieces of information; what unit? what shift? what job? where from? Once inside, talking ceased. Everyone would get down to business. No one wanted to waste what little time she was allotted.

Twenty plus women showered at a time. All herded into a changing room, where we'd strip, first our helmet, MOPP IV suit, gas mask, then regulation hospital gear, boots, and underwear, before proceeding into the showers, where hot water was never a guarantee. I never cared. In the heat and the sand and the wind and the sweat, even cold water felt good. For me, a shower made a real difference. The feel of water cascading down my body, sliding through my greasy hair, pouring over my sweat-soaked skin, washing away the sand, even temporarily, was the ultimate luxury. It revitalized, gave me strength and made me feel decent again, even though I seldom had clean clothes to put on afterwards.

Following my shower, I most often went right back to my tent and my cot, tried to write a few letters, maybe read a little, talk a little, listen to my Chicago or Fleetwood Mac tapes, read my Bible and pray, before falling asleep. I was usually too tired to do anything else. There was seldom anything else to do anyway.

There was a recreation tent, where a TV-VCR was available with a huge selection of video tapes families and friends sent, but I only browsed the bins. The recreation tent was also where they kept the large containers of stuff sent to "Anonymous Soldier." There we'd find bins filled with lotions, shampoo, and razors, hygiene stuff from corporations too. We never knew what we would find.

Occasionally, I'd hear about a vehicle going to the PX and hop a ride. The PX had limited open hours which seldom coincided with mine. When I couldn't go, I'd give a list of items to others who'd pick up stuff for me. People were very good about helping each other.

A trip to the PX also meant a trip to the phone tents. Located in the same general area, we could easily walk from one to the other. Phone calls home stirred the same mix of emotions that cards and letters did, only magnified, because you actually spoke to your loved one. The anticipation that built as you waited in line was almost unbearable. Your precious 15 minutes on the line flew by. You seldom had time to say all you had planned. And, in your heightened state of emotion, you often misinterpreted or misread the voice from back home on the other end. A negative call could throw you into depression and set you back for days.

Most days, I'd just go back to my cot and pass out. Sleep was multiply important. Without it, I couldn't function; without it I'd get sick. Above all else, I did what I could to maintain my health. Sleep, uninterrupted sleep, eight hours of uninterrupted sleep, was almost unheard of. Things exploding, banging, clanging, voices, generators, Scud alerts, howling wind, pelting rain, people bumping your cot, music, the high pitched whine of Muslim prayers five times a day, messages over the PA system, intruded mercilessly. After working twelve to thirteen hour shifts, seven days a week, I considered myself lucky if I averaged five hours of sleep each day.

Days off happened every two to three weeks. When mine came around, I'd spend them doing catch-up chores; wash clothes, answer mail and attempt to relax. Often, I'd just sleep. I'd try not to be too visible, because the military doesn't like idle people. If you didn't appear busy, someone would find something for you to do. There was always something that needed doing. They called it "other tasks"—jobs that we all were expected to do as part of living on a military compound. Tasks varied according to rank. Even so, I did my share of sand bagging, trench digging, tent building, concertina wire placing and watch duty, all after working a 12-hour shift.

Officer-in-charge (OIC) duty was considered part of the "other tasks." It was assigned on a rotation basis, and all officers had to comply when their turn came up. It was 24 hour duty during which the officer was in charge of the entire compound, everything: patients, EPOW's, hospital, all military personnel and equipment, including vehicles. The OIC was expected to be available and ready to make decisions, handle whatever came up every second of the 24-hour shift. The job was overwhelming and scary, but more than anything else, it required a lot of plain, old-fashioned common sense. There were always others of higher rank available to help.

February 20th was my lucky day to be OIC. It was my first day back to work after 36 hours in the ER with an IV drip pumping fluids back into my body. Two of my tent mates had taken me there after I'd passed out. The delicious chicken that I had savored three nights before, turned out to be tainted. Food poisoning was the diagnosis, although I wondered if they were keeping something from me when a priest showed up to give me the "Sacrament of the Sick." He came out of no-where; just showed up at my bed side. I appreciated the bless-ing. Stateside, the physical condition I left the hospital in would have gotten me a prescription for several days of bed rest. But, I was in the desert, in a war zone, and it was my turn to be OIC.

"Fire in the billets! Fire in the billets!"

"Oh, God! Please contain it," I prayed as I ran towards black smoke billowing from a tent smokestack on the other side of the compound. The pungent smell of burning fuel spread quickly. Sergeant Jackson, the armed Sergeant-of-Arms assigned to me as OIC, was at my side before I realized it.

"Tents are packed in so closely," he said, "if one goes up in flames, all could go."

"My thoughts exactly," I said. It's got to be bad to burn in this rainy sleet." He was two steps ahead of me as we ran towards the smoke.

"Rain'll probably keep the wind from spreading it," he said.

"Good point, let's hope so," I responded back, laboring to breathe in my weakened state. Rounding a corner we were brought up short. Like an Indian sending signals, a coughing soldier was balancing astride the smoking canvas tent roof. Smoke billowed beneath the blanket he held over the smokestack.

"What the hell is he doing?" asked Sergeant. Jackson.

"Looks like he's putting the fire out!" I said. "What I want to know is, how in Hell did he get up there?"

"Shimmied up the side, ma'am," came the explanation from a spectator. "Just like a monkey. Fantastic, Ma'am."

"Anyone hurt?"

"No ma'am."

"Suspect an improper mix of diesel fuel with water in the little furnace," was my explanation on the official report put on file. Diesel fuel plus water was known to cause flare ups. Fortunately, this one happened in the smokestack. All tent personnel had been warned when given the heat source. The furnaces—left over from the Korean War—had caused many such problems.

With that crisis averted and the report written, I returned to the hospital to work out the rest of my shift, praying that no other emergencies would occur during my OIC stint.

Later, Sergeant Jackson and I were making rounds, checking on vehicles, when we discovered that one was not secured. It was supposed to be locked and chained in a specific spot. We traced it to a tent on the other side of the compound where an unauthorized party was in progress. Inside, the tent was very dark. Squinting we could make out many bodies, coupled in various positions, engaged in non-military activities.

"All I want to do is address the problem of why the vehicle is not secured?" I shouted into the darkness. Bodies shifted, but no one said a thing. I turned to Sergeant Jackson. He asked, "How far do you want to take this, ma'am?"

"Right out the door," was my response.

We turned and left, never discovering the answer. Situations like this—that were never addressed militarily—occurred often. Right or wrong, that evening, we made a decision to find our answer elsewhere. I was glad to relinquish my position as OIC at the end of the shift.

The PX offered a respite from desert sands and all things drab and brown. Whenever possible, when I could find a free hour or two, I'd hitch a ride and wander from shelf to shelf drinking in familiarity. With eyes closed, I'd pretend that I was walking down an aisle in my Rini's Grocery Store, back in Ohio, shopping for dinner. Just the sight of American products lined up on shelves made me feel closer to my family and the home that now existed only in memory. I'd run my fingers over the familiar brand names, occasionally pick them up and put them back, straightening them on the shelves. Holding them I'd think, *See, there really is an America out there at the other end of the desert. It's not all a dream.*

Prayer sustained me in the desert. Not the daily ritualistic rattling off of memorized ditties, but deep down conversations with the Saints, God the Father, and Jesus Christ, in whom I believed. How different my faith was becoming. The furious, angry new recruit was regaining an enhanced sense of the importance of a belief beyond self, of a love that has no bounds, of the comfort that daily talks with a higher power can bring. I prayed from sunup to sundown, from one Scud alert to the next, from patient to patient and from Muslim chant to Muslim chant. In times of fear and triumph, my sweaty, often plastic covered hand, would instinctively clutch the cross around my neck or finger the rosary in my pocket. Silently I'd utter a few "Hail Marys."

Faith is a powerful magnet attracting those with like minds, like thoughts and beliefs. It was late January the first time we shared the Eucharist (Holy Communion) at KKMC. Word spread throughout the compound bringing a bunch of us together. We were not all the same denomination. None of that mattered. We were united by our Christian beliefs. We exchanged prayers, sang familiar songs and shared in Holy Communion.

News of our faith group spread, and soon we got wind of a Polish Mass that was to take place in the billets at KKMC. These doctors and nurses were stationed in an actual brick and mortar, stone hospital in the city. They were Polish civilians; doctors, nurses, and an anesthesiologist, members of a United Nations team that had been brought in to help in Saudi hospitals during the crisis. One of the nurses in our group spoke Polish, so she interpreted for us. Mass was beautiful. So different yet so familiar.

My faith was changing to one more childlike, accepting. Whatever was going to happen was going to happen. If I was going to die, then so be it. In the meantime, there were patients to care for and much work to be done.

Sometimes, in the midst of long, terrifying hours with missiles exploding over-head, caring for enemy prisoners under armed guard, performing exhausting tasks, all while living in primitive conditions, it was hard to remember life back home. When tired and depressed, I could almost convince myself that this war was the only reality I'd ever known. Often, I'd think I was losing my mind. I may well have, if I didn't know that others shared the same experience.

I was lucky to live in Sweet Sixteen, where we had two in-tent, resident psychologists who helped us through the tough times. For the most part, we tent-mates all got along well. But, people are people and occasionally tempers would flare. One gal had a cadre of male visitors who showered her with luxuries. She had her own electricity when the rest of us had to share one light bulb, and received gifts of fruit, lace, and clothing.

Day in and day out or night in and out, depending on what shift you were working, life became phases of work, try to sleep, work, try to sleep. It was intense. Iraqi Scud missiles made it so, bombers taking off made it so, enemy prisoners of war made it so, hundreds of sick and injured civilians from different cultures (Egypt, Iran, Saudi Arabia and Iraq) flocking to our hospital made it so. After the war, the fear of Scuds lessened but prisoners still needed attention, and the civilians kept coming. And the weather, sandstorms and windstorms and rainstorms, freezing cold nights followed by sweltering days, temperatures fluctuating from one extreme to the other, made it so. We prayed, we laughed, we screamed and yelled, we cried, sometimes we briefly lost our senses. But, there was always someone to lend a hand or advice or an arm around the shoulder, or a kind word. We were human beings caught up in war games in a foreign land, and we clung to each other, desperately.

CHAPTER NINE

"He fills me with strength and protects me where ever I go."

Psalm 18

On February 28th, President Bush declared victory and ordered a cease-fire. Three days later, on March 3rd, Iraq accepted the terms set by the coalition and the war was officially over. When the announcement came, we cheered!

"Attention! Attention! The area has been officially declared chemical free. I repeat. The area has been declared chemical free. MOPP IV equipment is no longer required. MOPP IV equipment is no longer required!"

The news was greeted with great excitement, although it took several days before we felt its effects. I can still remember the lightness, the elation, almost disbelief, as I removed the heavy MOPP IV outfit—gas mask, charcoal coat and pants, rubber boots and gloves—from my belt. Carefully, I folded everything and stuffed it into my trunk, expecting to feel a sense of relief. But, relief didn't come. That suit had been my only security; my only chance at survival. When it came time to close the lid on it, I couldn't do it. Before I knew what was happening, my hand, as if directed by a greater force, picked up my chemical mask and clicked it back onto my belt. I could not let it go.

We assumed that the end of the war would signal a slowing down of duties and our deployment back to the United States and home. But a lighter work load was not to be. As traffic increased on the highway outside the compound, so did the accidents. Word had spread that the Americans had free food and medical care. Patients continued to stream in from

131

the desert, military and civilians alike. Many were badly injured. Most were malnourished and starving. All came to us to be healed and fed.

The end of the war also brought a lessening of the rules. Although not encouraged to do so, we were allowed off of the compound, so, when the opportunity arose I jumped at it.

I was in the company of McCalley, a 91 Bravo nurse, (similar to an LPN) who worked in my intensive care unit, and a couple of Kuwait interpreters Ali, Jassim and Eman, all taking a five minute break, when conversation turned to what to do the next day. We all had the day off.

"I know, why don't we go golfing?" laughed Eman. He was an American Freedom fighter helping translate for the Kuwaiti government.

"No, I'd rather go to the museum or the theatre," I responded in an uppity manner, knowing that none of those places existed here. We all laughed.

"How about a shopping trip to KKMC?" asked Ali, looking toward me, but speaking to the two Kuwaiti interpreters. "We're allowed off of compound grounds, now." He eyed the interpreters, who affirmed the possibility with accepting winks, before looking back at me.

It took me about five seconds to think about it. "Sure!" I shouted. It had been so long since I'd been off the compound. I was ready for an adventure.

"Great!" exclaimed McCalley. "I'll sign for the vehicle and meet all of you around 0900, in the yard."

Fresh from our twelve-hour shifts, we were a sorry, exhausted lot, but energy-charged with excitement as the Humvee joined the early morning masses rolling down the highway to

KKMC. My nose burned from the intense heat, blowing dust and sand, mixed smells of gasoline and burning oil wells mingling with the odors of humans and animals, camels and goats, moving down the highway in both directions. It could have been a morning rush hour state-side, were it not for the nature of the traffic: tanks, five-ton trucks, semi-tracker trailers, Humvees, cars, buses, bikes, herds of farm animals and camels going every which way.

Once inside the city, there wasn't much to see or do. KKMC was primarily military, with buildings and housing built for war. Some shops lined the streets, and there was the market, but there were nowhere near as many shops as would be found in a traditional Arabian city. Even so, the streets were teeming with people, a mixture of many cultures and military personnel. Most Arabian men were garbed in traditional robes, the women in a dark blue or black trailing garment called a *qamis*, their faces were covered with a shawl. Then there were the workers in their blue uniforms. Drab colors blended into sand-colored walls. Pungent odors assailed the senses: unclean bodies, unusual spices, animals, and the ever present, burning oil-well smell. A shop here or there beckoned, but I really didn't feel like getting out of the car and walking around.

We drove on, eventually stopping at a small store and restaurant, hoping to get some lunch. It was so filthy inside, we decided that we really weren't *that* hungry. The store carried few supplies, mostly big barrels of beans and roots. It did, however, carry RC Cola, warm of course. We each bought a can.

After a few more turns, we ended up in front of a huge rectangular marble structure with a tall steeple adorned with the Moslem symbol. It was one of the many Mosques in KKMC. Ali jumped out and went inside. Returning a few minutes later, with water glistening on his beard, he smiled, looking refreshed. There must have been a bathroom inside, because he had washed his face.

"I feel like a new person," he declared jumping back into the Humvee. "We can now go where ever you like."

"How about Kuwait?" I asked.

"No! It's too far," said Ali, "almost 200 miles of un-friendly roads.

"But...," I started to argue.

"They haven't been cleared of mines and other possible means of sabotage, yet." said Eman. "We can't be sure we'd be safe."

"We're liable to get shot, lost or worse," added Ali, "and, you know how your military hates to lose bodies!"

Despite their words, I had the feeling we could've talked them into it, so, I turned to Jassim and asked her. "Do you want to go, Jassim?"

"No," came the reply. "Two women and two men...it's too risky. Besides, as the highest ranking officer, I don't want the responsibility."

Few took notice of us as were drove around. We were left to roam as we pleased.

As we drove, we talked, about spirituality, mostly. Ali and Jassim, tried to explain to me Mohammed and their will-ingness to die for Allah. And, I tried to explain Christianity and the story of Jesus Christ, to them. Kuwaitis are a different kind of Arab, different from the Saudis, Syrians or Jordanians.

They are more open, not threatened by western influence and an exchange of ideas between cultures. They have no religious patrols. Ali and Jassim made it very clear, however, that they wouldn't believe anything I said about Jesus Christ, and I, in turn, told them, I couldn't believe anything they told me about their God. "True Islamic teaching," I tried to explain, "from my understanding, is very Christ-like. They don't kill people. But, I don't see evidence of that here," I told them. They just nodded, unwilling to agree, listening politely. I never said that Christianity is best for everyone. It's not for them. The Resurrection just blows their minds. They can't even begin to conceive of it. And I, with western Islamic understandings, as read in newspapers back home, see little of the beauty of their faith.

At a market, outside of KKMC in the Emerald City, I lost my desire to continue shopping. Appalled at the way things were sold, I'd had enough. Vegetables were shriveled up from the heat and hanging meat covered with flies, lamb in particular, swung from hooks. I turned my head in disgust, my stomach flip-flopping, as if taking in food poisoning by osmosis. The scene brought back bad memories of trips to Tijuana. I couldn't watch as people lined up to make their purchases. "Let's go home," I said.

On the ride back to the compound, we stopped at the PX and made a few purchases. The interpreters expressed amazement at the continuous selection of goods found there. To me, the shelves looked sparse. With the war ended and troops in the process of being sent home, supplies weren't being re plenished.

We parted that day with handshakes and an exchange of heartfelt "thank yous." Our day outside the compound was over. It had been a break in routine, a respite in a sea of trauma, emergencies and orders. I was grateful, uncertain of when another break would come. I had no idea another would come so soon.

CHAPTER TEN

"Whenever God lays a burden on you he leaves an extra grace too."

Carol Kavalhuna

"I need help over here!," shouted Dr. Luther, an orthopedic surgeon, leading a stretcher into the ward, "got a bad one."

"I'll get it," I waved off Hughes and Wagner who were busy with their own emergencies. I was in charge of the unit that day and had just finished with another patient.

"God! What happened?" I asked looking down at a waif of a girl, who couldn't have been more than nineteen years old. "A near sever," he answered matter-of-factly. "A tire...blew up in her face. All this damned heat! Damn near took her arm off! I took care of the bone, stabilized it with pins. But, her radial, ulnar and brachial pulses are thready and..."

"Does she need a vascular surgeon?" I asked.

"I'd rather wait. Watch her for awhile. If you see she's losing perfusion in her hand, call me immediately." As Dr. Luther hurried out the door, I began checking her arm. It appeared okay for the moment. That all changed within twenty minutes. Her pulses became weaker, and I noticed color draining from her hand, all signs that she was losing perfusion. I put in a call for Dr. Luther.

Dr. Luther arrived immediately, a concerned look darkened his face. After a quick examination he declared, "Arteries and veins need to be reconnected and vessels restructured a.s.a.p. or she'll loose the arm. She needs to be Evac'd,

137

STAT!" Looking at his watch he said, "The night plane leaves in a few minutes."

"Think we can make it?" I asked.

"You'll have to! She's not going to lose her arm because of me," he said. "She can't go alone. She'll need to be heparinized every hour."

"I'll go," I said, without a thought to what my leaving would do to ICU. "Good!" he said, "She needs an RN."

I figured she would need about 1,000 units of Heparin—an anticoagulant that thins out the blood—every hour, and Morphine for pain. If we're lucky, this would keep the blood vessels open until we could get her to the nearest vascular surgeon, wherever he or she might be.

"I'll need orders," I said as Dr. Luther scribbled on a pad. Ripping it off the pad, he handed it to me, called for MPs and an ambulance to take the cot to the airstrip. Studying the paper, I shouted to Hughes, "You'll have to take over. I gotta go with this patient."

She followed me to the medicine chest protesting loudly, "you can't just up and leave!" Ignoring her, I grabbed for the medication ordered.

"You're in charge today!" she protested.

"Not any longer," I said hurriedly, "you are! Get another RN out of bed. I'm not leaving my patient! She needs an RN and I'm going!" I signed out three days worth of Heparin and Morphine, grabbed the bag of medical equipment and ran after the stretcher already loaded into a waiting ambulance. Before I could think twice or even pack a bag, I was on a plane headed for Landstuhl, Germany, wherever that was.

Timing couldn't have been better. We were barely inside the belly of the enormous C-140 aircraft when the door closed and preparation for take-off began. One of the nurses on duty helped secure my patient to a bottom hammock and pointed me toward a row of seats just as the "prepare for departure," signal blared over the intercom. Belted in and unable to do anything for a few minutes, I looked around in awe.

The C-140 was an enormous aircraft. A portion of the interior had been converted into a hospital ship. Most of the seating area had been replaced with hammocks, stacked three high, and filled with the severely injured. About 100 patients literally swung from the ceiling of the plane. Side seating had been replaced with cabinets for medical equipment. The only part that resembled another plane was the seating in the first four rows, with one exception. All the seats faced backward.

Once airborne, I joined the hospital staff on duty. The four flight nurses on duty welcomed an extra pair of hands, especially the hands of another RN.

For the first time I noticed the name of my patient. Semelsberry, Paula, from a Transportation Unit. Fortunately, she was still unconscious from surgery and the Morphine we'd pumped into her. If she were lucky, she would stay that way and not remember anything about this trip.

Working so hard on a patient and seldom even knowing his or her name, was the one thing that always bothered me about my job here. All these people came through my ward injured. We'd work on them and in many cases save their lives, and we'd never even know their names. Some, like Semelsberry, would be transferred on for further treatment, and we'd never know what happened to them. And, they would never know who it was that made the right decision at the right time that gave them their lives back. It wasn't that I or any of my colleagues wanted a pat-on-the-back for doing our jobs. It's just that if I were injured, I would want to know who saved me or helped me so I could at least say, "thanks," later on.

Swinging in the hammock two levels above Semelsberry was a young man who had a tracheostomy—a hole in the neck to allow him to breathe. He'd been hit in the face by a tank turret and couldn't breathe because of all the swelling from the fractured bones. Amazingly, he was conscious and *very* frightened. I talked to him, calmly, about everything and anything. He couldn't talk, of course, but he listened and relaxed a little.

There were many other patients, too, many heart attack victims, and young people with a multitude of complications and problems. Most slept, drugged by antibiotics prescribed for various reasons. Occasionally, one would scream out or moan in pain, need medication or a bed pan. Air pockets, pressure changes and the bumping of the flying plane affected injuries in a variety of ways. I climbed among the patients, talked, prayed and gave medication. And, once, every hour, I gave Semelsberry 1,000 units of Heparin and monitored her Morphine, praying all along that her vessels would remain open so her arm could be reattached.

The ten-hour flight to Landstuhl flew by. Startled by the, "prepare for landing," signal, I sat back down for the first time since take-off and contemplated where I was going. *Landstuhl. Where the heck was Landstuhl?* I knew it was in Germany but that's about all. And orders. *My God, I never got any orders!* For a moment I panicked. You don't go anywhere in the military without orders. *Well, apparently you do*, I thought. *No use worrying about it now.*

The back of the plane opened up onto a runway close to the hospital at Ramstein Airforce Base. Some patients were able to walk, but most, like Semelsberry, were taken out. I followed, glued to her stretcher.

Squinting, I walked out of the plane into the bright sunlight. Even though distance between the plane and the hospital was short, the colors were overwhelming; bright blue skies, white clouds, green trees, and multi-colored flowers lined the concrete walkway to the emergency room door. It took a mnute for my eyes to adjust. Drab browns, tans and military green were all they had seen for months. Crisp spring air startled my lungs, making me gasp and shiver for a few seconds. Desert air had registered 120 when I'd left.

Patients were processed through an emergency room where itineraries and orders, sent ahead, were waiting.

I met with the head nurse about Semelsberry, going over the chart of treatment given thus far. She put a call out for a Vascular surgeon, as an Orthopedic surgeon examined the bone repair. He agreed that it was a vascular problem and doubled the call for the Vascular doctor.

"Thank you, Lieutenant Kwiatkowski," he said, "you've done all that was necessary. We'll take it from here. You are dismissed." I saluted and walked out of the emergency room. It was such a let down. No closure. I'd been with Semelsberry for thirty hours straight. Thirty hours since I'd slept. Exhausted, I trudged down the hall, trying to decide what to do next. *Find the NCO and ask about getting back to Saudi,* my mind dictated. Thoughts were interrupted by a commanding voice.

"Lieutenant! Your uniform! It's a disgrace! What is the meaning of this?"

I turned slowly my hand responding in a salute, as trained, all the time thinking, "you jerk." I had to grit my teeth to keep from screaming at him. Choosing my words carefully, I explained why I looked as I did and how I had come to be in his hospital.

"I'm headed back on the next transport out," I said.

"Let me see your orders!"

"Sorry, sir. We left in such a hurry I wasn't given any." I responded.

He wasn't happy about my explanation, but he accepted it. He sent me to the Red Cross who supplied me with toilet articles and then on to an NCO who set me up in a room normally reserved for visiting medical personnel. "I'll do some checking and figure out how get you back to your unit," he said.

The room looked like the Taj Mahal to me. It had a bed—a real bed with a mattress and springs—and a shower and a toilet that flushed. *Pure luxury!* I was ecstatic! Peeling off my dirty clothes, I jumped into the shower letting hot water cascade down my exhausted body. With my eyes closed I imagined that I was back home in Ohio, in my own shower. In the cupboard I found clean hospital gowns; not too fashionable but good enough to walk my filthy castoffs down the hall to the laundry room. Collapsing into bed, I slept well, really slept, for the first time in many days.

"Paging, Dr. Duiven. Paging Dr. Duiven. Please call..." The loud speaker was unfamiliar. The blare jolted me out of a deep sleep. Willing my mind to focus, bed springs squeaked, as I slowly opened my eyes. *Where am I?* came the question from afar. Painted walls, a light fixture, windows with shades came into focus as slowly, I remembered.

Returning to Saudi turned out to be more difficult than I expected. It took more than three days before there was an available seat on the transport. In the meantime, I had no orders. Nowhere I had to be. So, I played. It was wonderful.

"Hello," came the familiar voice on the other end of the line.

"Hello, Tom. This is your gypsy wife. Guess where I am?

"Are you in the U.S.? Are you coming home?" he asked excitedly.

"No, nothing that good, not for another six weeks or so," I said. "I'm in Germany!"

What a luxury to talk to Tom privately, without a 15 minute limit and the pressure of others waiting in line. We talked for half an hour about Semelsberry, my other patients, about him, the kids, grandkids, other family members, friends, work, everything under the sun. Mary, our youngest, was excited about her Senior Prom that was coming up in a couple of weeks, he'd said. I blocked out the conversation knowing that if I listened too long, I'd be overwhelmed with sadness. She was ready to graduate, and I'd missed her entire senior year.

Tom said he'd been bugged by two *Plain Dealer* Reporters about when my unit would return. Apparently, after a local commander threw them out, they turned to him. It really was stressful for Tom. I assured him that I had no dates as yet, but that I would be home soon. Many Ohio units had already returned.

With clothes cleaned and pressed, I felt like a million bucks as I strolled outside. The air was chilly, but I barely noticed. It wouldn't have mattered if I did. I didn't have a jacket.

Colors, glorious colors were everywhere. It was late spring in Landsthul. Snow melting off the mountain tops created cold running streams. Lavender, gorgeous clouds of purple, blanketed the hillsides. Grass had already turned green, and flowers popped up everywhere—brilliant colors in immaculate beds. It was like discovering color in a black and white world. Cool crisp air assaulted my nostrils. I kissed the grass, smelled the flowers and ran my hands over the dew. I felt like a kid in a candy shop. So many things I had taken for granted.

Remstein Air Force Base was tucked into a valley, in the foothills of the Alps, near the town of Saarbrucken, on the French border. The base had played a major role in World War II, especially in the liberation of troops at the end of the war. Now it was servicing the Persian Gulf War personnel, mainly the injured. So, it came as no surprise that it also housed a PX, a very large PX Mall. Fortunately, one of the only things I'd had on my person when I left Saudi was my credit card, so with time to spare, I went shopping.

The PX Mall was similar to the many strip-malls found in America. It wasn't enclosed as most are, but did contain separate businesses, a giant department store, flower shop, jewelry shop and candy store all within the same area.

In the department store, I lingered in the perfume section getting high on the aromas, sampling them all, trying to remember what it felt like to be a woman again. My one big purchase was a bottle of Fendi cologne bought for me, just me, because I love it. In the flower shop I bought potpourri for the tent and in the candy shop, I splurged on candy for everyone; real German chocolate so good I can still taste it.

While at the base, I met two captains, one male, one female, also staying in the medical rooms beside mine. We ate a few meals together and shared a few laughs. They tried to talk me into going to Paris with them for a couple of days. It was tempting, but I couldn't chance it. Any day now, I'd get the call that there was room for me on the next transport out.

By the end of the second day, my body was reacting to the change in environment. Although I was able to catch up on some much needed sleep, the cool temperatures and mountain breezes played havoc with my immune system. Before I left Germany, I was well on my way to a full-blown case of bronchitis.

The third day, the NCO wrote up orders allowing me to get back into the war theatre. I'm not sure how he did it as it was still classified as a war zone. He must have had contact with my command there.

The plane going back was virtually empty. No stretchers swung from the rafters. Only a few seats, about half, were occupied. It was late April. The war had been over for almost a month. Units were being deployed home daily. All but mine. My comrades were still there, doing what they had done throughout the war. I was heading back, back to the war theatre where the only thing different was the lack of Scud missiles overhead and enemy prisoners of war. Everything else remained the same; a challenging, exhausting existence. This time though, it would be harder for me, because I had experienced a taste of freedom; a taste of the real world.

CHAPTER ELEVEN

"I, for one, know of no sweeter sight for a man's eyes than his own country."

Homer, The Odyssey

"We're moving," said Captain Reese

"What do you mean, moving?" I asked. "You mean going home?"

"No, Lieutenant Kwiatkowski, we're being moved to KKMC. The hospital there."

"What about the 251st?" I asked. "They going home? Don't tell me they're going home." I could feel the anger rising. Day after day troops were going home, and we were still here, working harder than ever. To add insult to injury, we had to give departure physicals to all of those being sent out, including the 251st. I was furious! "They come here and live in luxury villas while we eat sh.. and they get to go home before us?" It wasn't fair.

The next morning, we gathered our gear and were bused into the city to the luxury villas we'd heard so much about. They lived up to their reputation; running water, hot showers, beds with springs, real flush toilets, washers and dryers, and most important of all, air conditioning. May in the desert brought little rain, some sand storms and 120 temperatures. What a relief to be able to sleep in a real bed, in a real apartment, in air-conditioned comfort. It was heaven!

We were placed in the villas much as we'd been in the tent—officers together. This time, though, each three bedroom villa was shared by only six officers. In ours, from Sweet

Sixteen, came Hughes and Holmok, Hosslern and Wagner, Kocsis and me. Kocsis and I had a room and a door we could close for privacy. What a luxury.

The transfer to the KKMC Hospital did not release us from duty. Instead, our workload increased dramatically. Patients from our tent hospital were moved into the traditional brick hospital in the city, still under our care. There we continued to nurse them as before, but this time in unfamiliar surroundings with unfamiliar equipment. We still worked our twelve hour shifts. But, at the end of our shift, we were expected to go back to the desert camp and work additional hours helping to take down the tent city and pack it up for home. It was just as dangerous and back breaking as it had been putting it up. Each time floor boards were taken up the underside would be covered with scorpions and other lethal varmints. We had to be overly careful. In addition, the whole back breaking procedure was complicated by 120° heat.

I only made it through three days of the tear-down. One day in particular, we'd been working since dawn removing flooring, and stakes and taking down tents in the 120° heat, when I started to get dizzy. I'd covered myself with tanning lotion and had been drinking the prescribed amount of water, but the heat and the lifting got to me, and I almost passed out. I was so dizzy that I flagged down a Sergeant and told him I had to go back to the villa, immediately. He took one look at me and drove me back. Once inside the air-conditioned comfort of my room, I passed out and slept for more than twelve hours. I never went back to help with the removal. *Officers*, like myself, had put the tent city up, now it was the *Enlisted's* job to take it down. Besides, they [the enlisted] had been ordered to do it.

Transition to the hospital in KKMC was difficult. We were fortunate that there were some really wonderful people in the 251st. Even though they were preparing to leave, three nurses, two males and a female, would come over and help us when we were bogged down with all the Iraqi patients. One of the men had a family name that was common to my family. I tried to establish a connection. He was from South Carolina, and I knew that generations ago, my relatives were thrown out of England for tax evasion and some settled in South Carolina. Although we were never able to make the link up, it was a diversion and a fun thing to contemplate.

The hospital in KKMC posed a new collection of problems. The Arabs, especially the doctors, were arrogant and unskilled compared to U.S. medical teams. The nurses, many of them Egyptian, were much worse than the doctors. They attend nurses' school when they are fourteen and come out with an education comparable to a nurses' aide in the U.S. It was hardly enough training to qualify them for the jobs they held. Together with the Arab doctors, they made a lethal team. In addition, all the equipment was German. Many life-threatening procedures had to be done the old-fashioned way because we couldn't read or understand the directions on the machines. Their equipment was modern and up-to-date, if you could read German. It was maddening.

One of our added responsibilities was to perform exit or departure physicals on all those leaving the theatre. Eyes, hearing, skin, a regular physical had to be passed before a soldier would be allowed back into the U.S. The government didn't want any unknown rashes or diseases being brought back home. Knowing this, many soldiers lied about symptoms and minor health problems. No one wanted to be detained, even for a day, after his or her orders to leave arrived. This denial of symptoms would come back to haunt many a veteran, later.

Emotionally, I struggled with giving these physicals. Soldiers leaving, bubbled over with enthusiasm about the trip home. I was happy for them on the one hand, but at the same time angry that it wasn't our unit. Especially when the 251st got to leave before us. That really set me off. The closer we got to a window home, the harder it was to maintain a sense of composure.

Saudi guards, locked and loaded AK-47's ready for attack, guarded all the units in the hospital. They were on every floor. It was frightening to see them. Perhaps if we could have understood them, they wouldn't have seemed so imposing. They wouldn't have talked to or acknowledged me anyway. Although they respected the American military uniform, they didn't respect women in it, especially those women who happened to have red hair, blue eyes and were left-handed.

With all the Saudi protection, it was surprising that a young Iraqi, about twenty-one, was in the unit. His neck was broken. I was walking by his room when I observed a doctor and a nurse, Polish, I think, trying to put Crutchfield Tongs into his head. These tongs, applied correctly, stabilize vertebrae and prevent paralysis. The bed was in an upright position and the patient was struggling.

"What are you doing?" I demanded, walking into the room. The doctor ignored me pretending he didn't understand English. "This isn't the correct procedure! This guy is going to be paralyzed!" I tried to get him to put the bed down and get the kid some Valium to relax him. Normally, the area is anesthetized, tongs are put in, a bar comes around the back and you have traction to maintain the stability of the neck.

We exchanged angry words in our respective languages. I have no idea what he said to me.

"You're a fool! You're trying to kill this kid!" I shouted.

I stormed out of the room so upset that I could hardly contain myself. We had an excellent neuro-surgeon on duty who could have handled this correctly in two seconds.

I reported the incident up the chain of command, but it didn't matter. I don't know what happened to the young man. I'm sure he ended up a quadriplegic, if he's alive at all. The Saudi's didn't care. It was rumored that they played with patients—experimented. After witnessing that, I believe it.

The hospital in KKMC was huge, comparable to Metro-General, in Cleveland. It was equipped with the newest and best equipment, but lacked trained personnel to use most of it. The level of medical skill was frightening. Doctors receive little to no training that I could see. I saw enough to know that I didn't want to get sick in Egypt or Saudi Arabia.

American patients as well as the ones we brought from the tent hospital, were sent to our unit. One of the successes was the tetanus patient that transferred with us. Even though she was an Iraqi, she was never stable enough to send her on, so she remained under our care. Had she been transferred to the Saudis, she never would have made it. She was a living miracle. I never would have bet on her survival when she was brought in.

Tetanus causes seizures in the muscles. In the middle of seizures, she'd arch her head backwards touching her back. We had to paralyze and trach her and wait out the thirty days for the toxins to clear her body. Eventually, she walked out of the ward. It was a miracle.

Many of the American and Allied patients we were still getting had angina related illnesses, chest pains caused by dehydration. Occasionally, we'd get a really bad case. Vincent was one. Vincent was a Combat Engineer who'd gotten blasted by a terrorist bomb left behind for the clean-up crew. Combat Engineers clean up after the war is over. The blast was so strong, that it blew his boots off. He came in with burns covering his face, arms and legs, and injuries so substantial that he had to have brain surgery and was on a ventilator for a long time. The first thing he said when we took him off of the ventilator was, "I want to talk to my wife."

In the basement of the hospital was a telephone with direct line satellite hookup to the U.S. I decided that after what Vincent had been through, he deserved to have his wish granted. The long line waiting parted as I wheeled Vincent, an obviously messed up, seriously ill patient, into the room. "He's going first," I announced. "He needs to talk to his wife."

We got Vincent's wife in Colorado. He let her know that he was okay, and she did the same. After that, he recovered rather quickly, but he was still bootless.

On my next day off, I conned one of the Bell pilots we had befriended, who had a car, to take me on a mission to find size thirteen boots. We drove to several supply depots before we found some. Size thirteen is rather large and hard to come by, especially in a combat area where supplies were dwindling because troops were being deployed home. But, in a supply depot in the northern sector I went up to this Sergeant and said, "I need a pair of size thirteen boots!"

"Sure you do, lady," he said, laughing.

"Sergeant," I said with authority, "I said I need a pair of size thirteen boots for a guy that is hurt and by God, I'm going to get them for him."

Hesitantly, he asked, "Lieutenant, you got papers for them?"

"Sergeant, I'll sign anything you want me to sign. Now get me the boots!"

Vincent couldn't believe it when I walked into his room with size thirteen boots! Tears filled his eyes he was so grateful. Shortly thereafter, he was transferred to Germany, his first stop on the way to Colorado.

It wasn't all work in the hospital in KKMC. For the few brief moments during our day or night, there was a nurses' lounge to relax in. *Ha! Relax!* I laugh when I think of it. In the room was a television airing only government controlled programs. The only one I remember was an exercise program—"Aerobics"—with a guy demonstrating. Women are of no consequence, so it was geared strictly towards male fitness. We laughed at the gyrations of the host. *Hilarious!* The lounge also housed a snack bar with food not unlike the Saudi stuff we were fed in Dhahran when we first arrived. It was bad stuff. But, when you're hungry, you eat.

Many procedures over there reflect the Muslim faith, permeate every facet of society, especially medicine. Drugs and alcohol were strictly regulated because they were forbidden by religion. Therefore, any drugs or medication had to be signed out with two signatures, and then, the empty vials had to be returned. The three main drugs given for pain were Morphine, Codeine or Demerol. They used a lot of generic drugs, so we had to be very careful about getting and giving the right thing. There was no such thing as a "Physicians' Desk Reference," which is referred to all the time in the U.S. to make sure that side-effects and reactions are taken into consideration each time a drug is prescribed. Medical procedures used in the hospital in KKMC are 20 to 30 years behind standard American medicine. We managed, but it was scary. After only a few days in the KKMC hospital, I no longer envied the 251st. They may have had air-conditioned villas to live in, but work for them must have been Hell!

Each day in KKMC brought us closer and closer to our window home. As the days progressed, life in our villa became more intense.

Tempers flared more than usual. Holmok became even more psychotic and maternalistic. Her method of control was to set an arbitrary curfew, and if we weren't in by the time on her clock, she'd lock us out. It was ridiculous. Hughes was so fed up one night that they got into a knock down, drag out fist fight. In the end, Hughes moved into our room leaving Holmok alone, which was her agenda all along.

Through CNN and the radio we learned that returning troops were being given a "hero's welcome" all over the country. It should have made us feel good, but it didn't. We started having regular counseling sessions in our villa about the whole "hero" concept. None of us felt like we deserved that kind of praise. We all, each in our own way, had to come to grips with the whole idea that some folks thought we were "heroes."

The "hero" thing was just the tip of the iceberg, however. For months each of us had repressed emotions. Now that the fear of death was over and deployment home was right around the corner, these repressed emotions came bubbling to the surface.

Thoughts of what we'd been through replayed in our minds. *How'd I do that?* I'd ask myself. *How'd we do that?* you'd ask your colleagues. Kocsis, the psyc nurse, put it into perspective in a way that I could accept and understand. She said that we had sacrificed our lives by coming over and doing our jobs. That we didn't whine or complain or try to get out of our duty. We did our best as was asked of us. In that sense, we sacrificed or time, our lives and our families for the unknown. It may not fit our own internal concept of what a "hero" is, but we must accept the fact that in others' eyes, we do qualify. I tried my best to accept that approach. It was very, very difficult.

As time to return to the U.S. came nearer, thoughts of primping and making oneself presentable again began to sur-face. None of us wanted to go home looking as we did; dried-up skin, sun bleached and dried hair, make-upless. I decided to freshen my hair color so I went into KKMC to a Saudi store and picked up a box of Miss Clairol Hair Color in the only color they had, black, of course. Black sounded good to me, especially since it would cover the gray that had invaded my head.

Carefully following the directions, I applied my new hair color and eagerly looked into the mirror. "Oh my god!" was my first reaction. It was awful! Marlene did a double-take trying hard not to laugh. Everyone else in the villa gave off-handed, insincere compliments. The color was a bit extreme, I had to admit. Saudi black wasn't exactly complimentary on me. Eventually, I grew to except it. What choice did I have? It gave us all a lot of laughs, later.

In the hospital, nurses were known as "sisters"...like nuns. It was really weird and hard to get used to. As a woman, your military title made no difference to the Saudis. Even though the hospital Supervisor was British. He had been there so long—almost 18 years—that he too espoused Arabic thinking related to women.

In the hospital, I met a man from Jeddah who gave me his prayer chain. He wanted to take me to Jeddah to show me around and couldn't understand that I couldn't just leave; that I had obligations, a job in the hospital. A woman, committed to something was beyond his comprehension.

When word came that we would probably be leaving by May 30th, I didn't even get excited. Word came from my captain, while I was working. "Really!' I said without feeling. "I'll believe it when my foot hits the floor of the airplane and it takes off!" I said without blinking.

My reaction surprised me. I guess it was because my needs were finally being met—we had air-conditioning, a real bed and showers—and all of us in the villa were finally getting on well together. I had been thinking that if I had to, I could stick it out another couple of months. Besides, it *was* hard to believe. So many rumors had been circulating, even from command. At one time I kept a "rumor list." It got thrown out after the 87th rumor was recorded. Command would always be apologetic, "Well, sorry. We misunderstood what was said." At this time, I couldn't take another rumor.

The second week in May we were told that our window would definitely be Memorial Day weekend. It gave us plenty of time to prepare, although I could have and would have gotten on that plane with just the clothes on my back. We were all issued desert BDUs to wear home. They were of an attractive tan camouflage fabric. It was a riot trying to get my whole last name, Kwiatkowski, stitched onto the badge. The seamstresses, men who ran the PX, had huge sewing machines. One of them did it for me.

When word got out that most of the Americans were pulling out in a few weeks, the capitalist Arabs, Bedouins and anyone else with stuff to sell, showed up at the PX with their wares. It became a giant flea-market. I bought Arab cologne and shampoo and anything else I could afford. I looked for a chess set, but they apparently don't play chess in Saudi Arabia.

Reality started to sink in that we were really going home this time, and I started to worry about how I looked. I had dyed my hair that gawd-awful black, a few weeks earlier, and started to primp again. Would Tom find me attractive? I had lost a great deal of weight, and my pants just hung on me. I tried to convince myself that it wouldn't matter to him. That he loved and missed me, not my body. But the package returning was very different from the one he left months ago. The thought of seeing him again and renewing our physical life got me very excited. I felt like a virgin. After six months of celibacy, I had to work to get the juices flowing again.

I was so grateful to be leaving this awful country. Then, I'd think about the Kurds. We, the U.S. promised we'd help them fight Saddam and then left them. My heart went out to them. I'd think about some of my patients and the foreign friends that I'd made and become sad. Then, in a blink-of-an-eye, I'd be ecstatic again. My emotions bounced back-and-forth, from one extreme to the other. I got really self-centered when it came to leaving a bad place.

Part of the preparation of leaving included several awards ceremonies put on by the Saudis—not the ones we worked with but the political element. They awarded us gifts and trinkets. They set in motion the Humanitarian Award which takes a long time to get through Congress.

One by one each officer—about 100 of the 300—were called up onto a makeshift stage by name, where a Saudi Prince shook our hands and thanked us for helping them in their time of need. They were very, very humble. When my name was called, the guy pronounced it correctly, explicitly, distinctly. He must have been a linguist because no one ever gets my name right. Everybody clapped and cheered. The ceremony was followed by a reception of fruit and punch and all kinds of "goodies."

"Hey Kwiatkowski, look at your certificate! Did you look at it?" asked Kocsis. Hughes, Hosslern stood with Kocsis, waiting. I glanced down at it an we all started to laugh.

"Nice work, Mr. Dianah Kwiatkowski!" laughed Hosslern. "Mr. Hughes, Mr. Kocsis and I, Mr. Hosslern, all agree," she added.

Right down to the ceremony, the Saud's refused to acknowledge, even on paper, that women, women from the Allied nations had helped save Kuwait.

The actual day of departure will be forever embedded in my memory. Duffels and footlockers had been packed and sent ahead to a giant airplane hangar where they would be inspected for contraband items not allowed into the U.S. Following in buses, once inside the hangar, we claimed our belongings, laid them out on the floor and waited while first one officer and then the MPs inspected each piece. If anything was found, AK-47's, grenades, 45 pistols, etc., the whole unit was held back. There were checks and balances, military style. Following inspection, we re-packed our bags and left them in a huge pile to be loaded onto the plane.

Emotions were running high. Grady had to say "good bye" to one of the Bell pilots with whom she had a special friendship. She was hysterical. These pilots had been so kind to a group of us, letting us use their apartment, take a bath, wash clothes, cook a real meal. We all had trouble saying, "good-bye." They were at the airport scheduled to take off on a routine mission, around the same time as our flight. We were going home. They would remain in Saudi for at least another year.

How fitting it was that our last day in Saudi would be our American holiday of Memorial Day—a day set aside to remember those who fought for our country. A special mass was held that evening and I'll never ever forget it.

Fifty plus people were squeezed into a makeshift room where an altar, made out of plastic 2-liter bottles, was adorned with a white sheet, on which two candles burned in holders on either side of the Eucharist elements. We gathered to give thanks for surviving the horrific experiences we'd all been through. We gathered to remember and give thanks for those who did not survive. The dynamic priest reminded us that each and everyone was leaving a bit of themselves here, in the desert, in Saudi Arabia. Much as a snake sheds its skin or sheep its coat of wool, each of us had shed a former self. I knew that the Lieutenant Kwiatkowski that arrived a few months ago, was very different from the one packed up and ready to head home. That priest's dynamic presentation remains with me to this day, and causes me to pause each Memorial Day to reflect, remember and give thanks.

The huge TWA 747 was loaded throughout the night while we slept wherever we could find space on the floor, benches, anywhere. No one complained. No one minded. We were going home.

Buses once again transported us, this final time, to the airplane. We filed out single file, lined up and waited for the signal to board. It was very, very quiet. No one spoke or screamed or carried on. Once on board, our seats were not assigned.

My final duty in Saudi was as Administrative Officer of the day, so I had to make sure that everything was going as planned. After everything and everyone was loaded, I met with the pilots and sat in the cockpit with them for much of the trip to Rome. For the rest of the trip, I don't even re-member who occupied the seats on either side of me.

No one cheered when the plane took off. Everyone was very solemn. We were all as numb leaving as we had been arriving. No one could believe that we were really going home. Those in window seats gazed out at the sunrise. Some took pictures. No one could deny that the Saudi desert did have spectacular sunrises. Even so, I remember thinking that, that was the last f...... Saudi sunrise I'd have to see.

Once airborne, the TWA stewardesses, in their naivete, turned on an Arabic movie, causing an immediate revolt. Or-anges flew through the air.

"Turn that damned movie off or they'll tear the TV moni-tors down," I yelled to the stewardesses who scurried toward the video monitor switch. The plane quieted down once again until the pilot made another announcement.

"I want all of you to know that we just cleared Saudi airspace!"

For the first time, everyone cheered and clapped and hollered! Our whole unit, all 300 of them, less a trail party of 50 who had to stay back to take care of the trucks, was on that plane. Finally, it was beginning to sink in that we were really going home.

Our flight made a fuel stop in Rome and another stop at JFK International, in New York City, where we were allowed to deplane and touch U.S. soil for the first time. It was overwhelming! Crowds of people had gathered and gave us our first taste of "hero worship." A stranger hugged me and welcomed me home.

We headed first for the phones to call family and tell them we were on U.S. soil. And, then to the fast food stands for a beer and a burger. I chugged a Miller Lite and slowly ate a burger, afraid of what both might do to my system. I was buzzed after only one drink.

The last leg of the trip, to Dayton, Ohio, was the hardest. We were all so excited to get home and yet all too aware that the camaraderie shared the last several months was coming to an end. That special camaraderie built through fear and pain and struggle, would never be the same. We all felt it.

Many struggled with the whole concept of coming home. For whatever reason, some did not want to be on that plane. Military life is easier in some respects. You are told what to do and when. Your basic needs are taken care of for you. Even your leisure time is restricted. For some, that life held more promise than the one to which they were returning.

I was overwhelmed with sadness for what I was about to lose. I had changed. My priorities were different. I'm different. Would I be able to cope with civilian life? With making my own decisions again? With freedom? Would my family and friends like the new me? All these thoughts swirled in my brain as we touched down.

When the door opened, the band played, "God Bless America," as we filed out of the plane. We were sectioned off, band on one side and families on the other. I saw Tom's head in the crowd and waved; my stomach, the beer and the burger churning. All I could think of, while waving madly, was the hell he'd been through while I was gone and how much he'd aged. I was sure he was thinking the same thing about me.

When the signal was given, I ran to him and kissed and hugged him, never wanting to let go. It was then that I realized that he wasn't alone. My whole family, kids, grandkids, sister and brother-in-law had all driven the three hours to greet me. All but David, my son who'd been in the Persian Gulf. He had returned states-side in March and couldn't get a weekend pass from San Francisco to come welcome me home. I understood. Mary had dumped her prom date to come. She'd gone and left early so that she could be here.

Family wasn't the only ones there. Some of the members of our unit who'd had to come home earlier were also there to greet us. It was a wonderful show of support.

From the airstrip we went to a motel to spend time with family. The thing I remember saying to my husband, once we got in the car and I told him I loved him, was, "I hate those f..... Arabs...not just Iraqis, the whole Arab culture!" I ranted and raved for a few minutes, not knowing what I was saying. Tom was Mr. Calm, letting me vent. I felt as if I were in a fog. I guess I needed that.

We had a nice dinner with everyone, swam, talked and cried a lot. It was a wonderful evening. The next morning, I boarded a bus with the rest of my unit, for Fort Ben in Indiana, where we would be out-processed. That process would take a week or more, after which I could go home to stay.

Out-processing involved debriefing and a physical. I had been sick so many times in Saudi that I wanted some extra tests done to make sure I wouldn't have any lasting effects from the desert. I was especially concerned with silicone problems from all the sand I know we'd inhaled. The doctors gave me a hard time about it. It was always my unit's fault for not having this record or that record. I insisted, however, in having tests run. Consequently, when my unit was released in early June, I was kept much longer. I demanded certain tests which they were slow to follow through on. I refused to leave, forcing them to deal with me. I'd stay at the base and occasionally spend weekends visiting with Tom. Sometimes I'd drive from Ohio for my appointments. Finally, on July 13, 1991, I was officially out-processed and could go home to stay.

"Sleep, riches, and health, to be truly enjoyed, must be interrupted."

Jean Paul Richter

"Flower, Fruit and Thorn"

My house was filled to over-flowing with friends and family attending a "Welcome Home" party. The noise of party-goers echoed from the living room, while I sat in the kitchen gazing at the medal, recently awarded to my Uncle Charlie, for service in Berlin during World War II fifty years earlier. There were tears in his eyes as he watched me admire it. My other uncle, who had also served in WWII, and a cousin and a friend who had served in Vietnam, looked on. Not a whole lot was said. Words didn't seem necessary. The medal transported each of us into battle in our respective wars.

Occasionally the door would swing open and someone would shout, "Hey Dianah, get in here. There's someone who wants to talk to you." I'd wave them off, not wanting to move. Strangely, I felt more comfortable with these old war veterans than I did with the others. It didn't seem to matter that we served in different wars, from different decades. In many respects, even though their wars were much worse than mine, we shared a common bond: one of camaraderie in battle, in fear, in desperation; one of being tested beyond our limits. One of survival when others did not. One of the love of freedom and this great country of ours. And one of coming home, unable to explain to those we loved what had happened to us. For many who were not there, the Persian Gulf War was not a "real" war. I don't know how many times I heard someone say, "It was only 21 days long. You were a nurse, you weren't in battle. What's the big deal?" It made me angry. How many car wrecks do you need to be in before it impacts you? One is enough, isn't it? How many Scud alerts does it take to create memories that reverberate terror? How do you explain that in a war with no front line everyone is in the battle? But with these family members, I did not need to justify or explain that. Long before, as a child, I had gravitated towards these same uncles at family gatherings as they shared their war experiences and had wished that girls could go to war. Now, forty years down the road, here I was part of them.

I wanted to believe when I came home that everything would be the same. It was, and that made it more frustrating. Everything was the same but me. Events, concerns and happenings that I had attached so much importance to before, now seemed trivial. Compared to the life and death struggle in Saudi, these daily events came up short. Emotionally, I didn't know how to handle it. I didn't know how to switch gears.

Strong, compassionate Dianah had become intolerant. I had to be so careful. Without even realizing it, I was trivializing others' concerns. This was not the me I had known for forty-seven years. I struggled to discover who this new person was.

On the outside, I projected a facade of the old Dianah: the one that everyone expected, knew and loved. The always in-charge, together Dianah. But, internally, I felt completely out of control. I was falling apart. My life had flipped 180 degrees from the army controlling every second of my day, to me controlling myself. And, I was painfully aware that I was not in control, not the way I used to be. Going back to work was good therapy. My colleagues welcomed me back with open arms. What was difficult was to be immersed in definitive roles—the strict adherence to what a doctor does and what a nurse does. After six months of being in a crisis mode each day, where you did what you had to do, it was difficult waiting for the right person to do "x" job when I knew I could jump in and do it myself, whatever "it" was. Anger was building. I was so proud of my husband and kids for going on with their lives, on the one hand, but, on the other hand, I was angry at all I'd missed. I was angry at so many things: the military and the many areas in which they were inept; the incompetent commander I'd served under; ill-maintained equipment and a lack of sufficient security in the unit in KKMC; and most deeply—I was angry that I'd been unable to change the "big picture" there.

For awhile I tried to do it alone. Tempers flared. My dear husband and kids put up with a great deal of emotionalism. Then, finally, one day while working with a patient who began having flashbacks from Vietnam, I realized that I was having all the same "post traumatic war syndrome," symptoms as he. I sought help immediately and began to mend.

My faith returned ten-fold. It was a pleasure being back home in my parish, attending Mass and going through the daily rituals. They helped me. The only time I clashed over my faith was when the priest mentioned Jesus, the Lord, the Allah, in his weekend sermon. I had to point out to him that my God is not Allah. I had heard and seen what Allah was all about, and he was nothing like Jesus Christ the Lord. Allah wasn't about redemption and love.

For me, the struggle has been to bring redemption to an ugly scenario. Saddam Hussein was wrong to invade Kuwait and we were right to be there to help. This I believe. But still I search. Maybe it's because my faith saved my sanity while I was there that I'm driven to find the meaning. Or maybe it's because my faith points the way to another redemption that was brought about 2,000 years ago when one man died a horrible death.

I believe that there are no coincidences in life. In the greater scheme of things, I needed to go to Saudi Arabia. I needed to experience all that I did in the way that I did. I needed to change. The "why?" still isn't clear to me. I'm still seeking direction for what it all means. Perhaps sharing my story is the beginning.

God Bless you and The United States of America.

And thank a veteran for your freedom.

Lieutenant Dianah Kwiatkowski, now Captain Kwiatkowski, is still serving as a nurse in the Army Reserves. She continues to work in the Ohio hospital she left when deployment orders came. Along with her husband, Tom, she resides in the Ohio area with their five children, many grandchildren and friends. Captain Kwiatkowski, came home a changed woman with an eye on the day she would fulfill her military obligation. But her promotion to Captain and ensuing years of personal growth within the military, led her to believe that her nursing expertise as well as her Desert Storm experience, are valuable assets. Now, more than a decade later, on Active Alert for deployment to Iraq, an aftermath of the terrorist attack on the World Trade Center, she is determined as a Captain in the United States Army, to do whatever is necessary to protect and preserve the rights and freedoms of this great country for her grandchildren and their children.

Her philosophy can be summed up in the words of Abraham Lincoln, "Let us have faith that right makes might; and in that faith let us to the end, dare to do our duty as we understand it." Kwiatkowski believes that one person can make a difference. She is making a difference.

Thank God for Captain Dianah Kwiatkowski and the thousands of men and women like her, willing to lay down their lives to preserve freedom for all of us and generations to come.